SPICE UP YOUR LIFE

Jonathon Aspey

SPICE UP YOUR LIFE

The Story of Liverpool's 1990s Renaissance

First published by Pitch Publishing, 2023

Pitch Publishing
9 Donnington Park,
85 Birdham Road,
Chichester,
West Sussex,
PO20 7AJ
www.pitchpublishing.co.uk
info@pitchpublishing.co.uk

ISBN 978 1 80150 381 5

Typesetting and origination by Pitch Publishing

Printed and bound in Great Britain by TJ Books Limited, Padstow, Cornwall

Contents

Foreword and Acknowledgements

WRITING *SPICE Up Your Life* has been a dream of mine for the last ten years. Since I began writing about football from a historical point of view, I'd dreamed about being able to write a book. I've written about many topics in the world of football, but none have really struck me like any of my writing about Liverpool Football Club. I don't particularly consider myself a Liverpool fan – or indeed of any English football club – but I have a love and appreciation for the history, fans and culture of Liverpool that far exceeds my passion for any other football club. So much writing about Liverpool is centred on the dominant periods of the 70s and 80s, and undoubtedly many books will be written about the ongoing period that Jürgen Klopp manages the club – hopefully for a long time to come – but the 90s remains a relatively forgotten period, despite the decade's importance in bringing the club to where it is now.

I'd like to firstly thank everyone at Pitch Publishing for deciding to publish this work. Again, this has been a dream of mine for quite some time, and it's frankly surreal to have that dream be realised. Secondly, I'd like to thank my wonderful wife for being a constant support to me throughout the writing of this book, and especially over the last few months following the birth of our wonderful daughter, taking her on days out with her grandma to give me a few free hours to focus solely on *Spice Up Your Life*. Without your support, this wouldn't have been possible. I know me saying, 'I need to write the book' so often hasn't always been easy. To my daughter, I hope you inherit my complete and utter obsession for football as you grow up, and I hope that one day you enjoy reading this. I did once try to write the book with you in my arms, but you wriggled far too much.

I'd also like to thank my grandad, whose interest in football I clearly inherited. Your devotion to Sunderland Association Football Club remains admirable. I'll always be glad we saw a match at the Stadium of Light together. Thank you for always asking about the book when we see each other, and thank you for keeping anything you read to do with Liverpool in case it helped! Many of my happiest childhood memories are of kicking a ball around with you and, although we can't do that anymore, I hope that you reading this book is one big happy memory that we can share.

Mum and Dad, thank you for always supporting me with anything, for telling me that I'm capable of doing anything, and thank you for being so proud of me when

I told you I was being published. Thank you for always asking about how the book is going, and I hope that you're proud of having your own copy of the book, even though neither of you particularly care about football. Mum, I'm sorry the book isn't all about David Beckham.

Finally, to you the reader. Thank you so much for picking up a copy of this book. I hope that the effort I went to in researching and writing this book was enough, and I hope that you enjoy reading about the 'Spice Boys' era of Liverpool Football Club, and the role that one man played in helping to recover the heart and soul of a football club in peril. YNWA.

Thank you.

Introduction

LIVERPOOL FOOTBALL Club is special. Whether you're a fan of the club or not, the esteem in which it's held in the eyes of football fans across the world is simply undeniable.

Since Bill Shankly arrived at the Merseyside club in 1959, it has relatively consistently been at the top of English football and remains so to this day as the Reds compete for domestic and European honours on a regular basis. Jürgen Klopp manages a team that plays a wonderful and successful brand of football loved by millions, and names such as Mohamed Salah, Roberto Firmino, Trent Alexander-Arnold and Thiago Alcântara are respected across the globe as Liverpool players.

It hasn't always been this way though. Liverpool haven't always been a top team competing for the Premier League, and their recent success marked the end of a long run of 30 years without winning the top domestic trophy in English football. Prior to that victory, amid the turmoil of the coronavirus pandemic in 2020, Liverpool's last league championship came in 1990 under then manager Kenny Dalglish. The years before that win had been tumultuous for the club, as they underwent a brief rebuild following the promotion of Kenny Dalglish to player-manager in 1985. In the five years following Dalglish's appointment, the club would once again dominate English football with a new team that featured John Barnes, Peter Beardsley and John Aldridge, and played delightful attacking football. The club – and city – would also experience the shocking tragedy of Hillsborough in 1989, an event that affected the club and those involved with it more than can ever be put into words. By the time Dalglish resigned in 1991, and Graeme Souness had experienced three years in the Anfield dugout, the club was in severe decline, going through the same kind of experience that Manchester United have in recent years following the retirement of Sir Alex Ferguson. A mid-table finish in 1993/94 wouldn't have been a ridiculous expectation had Souness not stepped aside.

Of course, Liverpool recovered, and once again became a top team in English football. This book, *Spice Up Your Life: Liverpool, the 90s and Roy Evans*, is the story of the key first stage of that revival under Roy Evans, a man who embodied the spirit of the club, and who might not have won any league titles during his tenure as manager from January 1994 to November 1998, but he gave the club its identity back and brought through several players who would bring the club back to prominence and are loved by the Anfield faithful to this day. This book gives Roy Evans the credit he rightfully deserves, salvaging the Reds in the mid-1990s and creating one of the most entertaining teams in the history of English football. If you have any doubt about that statement, watch Evans's Liverpool vs Kevin Keegan's Newcastle United from April 1996.

This book is also a love letter to a club I adore. Many of my happiest memories of watching football involve Liverpool, even though I don't necessarily consider myself a Liverpool fan. Writing this book over the last year has been a wonderful experience, and this is a story I feel needs to be told. This is *Spice Up Your Life: Liverpool, the 90s and Roy Evans*.

Chapter 1

Time Goes By – Liverpool Under Souness

ON THE morning of 22 February 1991, at a press conference held at Anfield, Kenny Dalglish stepped down as manager of Liverpool Football Club. Up to tht point, Dalglish had held the most prestigious job in English football since taking over as player-manager in 1985 and had continued the dominance of the Merseyside club. His tenure had included quite possibly the most triumphant season in Liverpool's history in 1987/88 – with a team featuring John Barnes, John Aldridge and Peter Beardsley playing scintillating football – as well as guiding the club through the traumatic 1988/89 season, the Hillsborough Disaster and the last-minute collapse against Arsenal at Anfield on the final day of the season.

Despite that moment, under Dalglish Liverpool had remained the top club in English football and the

Liver Bird was well and truly entrenched on its perch. Despite the improvements being made by teams such as Sir Alex Ferguson's Manchester United and Howard Wilkinson's Leeds United, there was little sign that this would change. After all, Liverpool had been dominant in English football for over 15 years. Liverpool chairman Noel White stated that he'd tried everything possible to keep Dalglish at the club, including offering him a break, but the reigning Manager of the Year would later go on to credit the emotional toll of the Hillsborough Disaster with playing a major part in his decision. Long-time coach Ronnie Moran was installed as caretaker manager, but he made it clear to the Liverpool board that he didn't want the job full-time. The search was on, with Phil Thompson and Alan Hansen the early bookies' favourites at 4/1 and 5/1 respectively.

On 16 April, however, club legend Graeme Souness was appointed manager. Souness had experienced considerable success as manager of Glasgow Rangers, winning three league titles in Scotland, as well as competing in Europe. Despite being a club icon, Souness had a reputation for his fiery personality and combative nature, which he maintained as a manager just as much as he had as one of the most gifted midfielders of his generation. Souness started well, with successive wins against Norwich City and Crystal Palace at Anfield, but two straight away defeats against Chelsea and Nottingham Forest handed the league title to George

Graham's Arsenal, and Liverpool went on to finish second in the First Division.

However, much of the concern surrounding Souness's early days in charge related to the future of several key figures at the club. Peter Beardsley – who had so effortlessly replaced Dalglish as the creative hub linking midfield to attack – had started the 1990/91 season in peerless form, but Dalglish's signing of David Speedie had cost him his place, with his future at Anfield now looking precarious. Speedie himself then found his own position under threat, with Souness linked to Mo Johnstone of his former club Rangers, and Dean Saunders of Derby County. With the possible departure of Beardsley, along with the retirement of Alan Hansen in March, it was becoming clear that change was afoot for the Reds.

As the summer of 1991 progressed, it was clear that the change that was needed at Liverpool was coming extremely quickly under Souness. Kop favourite Peter Beardsley was informed that his services would no longer be required at Anfield and was shockingly sold to Merseyside rivals Everton for £1m. Beardsley might have lost his place under Dalglish, but he still possessed the quality required to play in the famous red shirt, as he would show most memorably with Kevin Keegan's Newcastle United after joining in 1993. Beardsley claimed that then Everton manager Howard Kendall had admitted he never believed Liverpool would make him available. It was the first mistake Souness would make with personnel and was a pattern that would repeat itself again and again during the Scot's time in the Anfield dugout. What exacerbated the mistake was the fact that Beardsley was being moved out of the club, so that Souness could spend a then national record fee of £2.9m on Dean Saunders, who had scored 17 goals in 1990/91 for a relegated Derby County team. Saunders had been linked to Aston Villa, Nottingham Forest and – ironically – Everton before signing to partner the great Ian Rush for 1991/92.

Also making his way to Anfield from the Baseball Ground was centre-back Mark Wright for £2.2m – a record sum for a defender in English football. Another addition was Rangers' Mark Walters for £1.25m. On their way out of the club along with Beardsley were David Speedie – Dalglish's final signing – to Blackburn Rovers, Gary Gillespie to Glasgow Celtic for £925,000 and, perhaps most surprisingly, Steve Staunton to Aston Villa for £1.1m. Staunton had featured consistently for the previous three seasons, and many of the Anfield faithful questioned Souness's decision to part with the 22-year-old. As the 1991/92 season began, Liverpool fans had more reason to be concerned about the on-field performances than they had done for a considerable amount of time.

Liverpool opened the league season at Anfield against the previous year's winners of the Second

Division, Oldham Athletic. Souness's first league line-up featured Grobbelaar, Ablett, Burrows, Nicol, Whelan, Wright, Saunders, Houghton, Barnes, McMahon and the first start for young Steve McManaman, who would go on to excite Anfield throughout the decade. Liverpool went in at half-time 1-0 down following a scrappy sixth-minute goal from Earl Barrett, but a fantastic second-half performance from Ray Houghton gave them the win to start the season. However, a 2-1 defeat away at Maine Road against Manchester City followed, with the bright spot being the performance of McManaman, who sctruck with a diving header to bring the score to 2-1 and created the attack that gave Liverpool the chance to draw level from the spot; however, star signing Dean Saunders hit the bar. John Barnes and Mark Wright went off injured on a frustrating night for the Reds. Barnes would be out until January. To make matters worse, Ronnie Whelan went off injured in the next league match, a 0-0 draw against a Luton Town team that had finished 18th the previous season. Adding further salt to their wounds, Steve McMahon was also suspended following a red card received during the Luton match. It had been a frustrating start to the campaign, and it was the last thing that Souness needed.

Liverpool got back on track following that result, winning three straight matches, against Queens Park Rangers, Notts County and, most significantly, the Merseyside derby against Everton at Anfield, which saw Dean Saunders score his second goal of the season after he'd opened his account against QPR. Against the Toffees, Liverpool were 1-0 up within a minute through David Burrows and never looked threatened as they cruised to a 3-1 win. It was easily their best performance of the season so far and McManaman was fantastic once again. Despite an inconsistent start to the season, at this point Liverpool sat second in the table, one point behind Sir Alex Ferguson's Manchester United.

Reality stuck hard, however, as Liverpool then stumbled to only two wins in the next ten league matches up to the end of November, with losses to the unbeaten Leeds United and to Crystal Palace accompanying six draws representing 12 points dropped. Ian Rush also picked up an injury and would be out for several months. Liverpool's main culprit was their away form, with their win against Notts County being one of only two away league victories in the first half of the season. By the end of November, Liverpool sat 9th in the table, 13 points off Manchester United at the top.

In better news, in October Souness pulled off a fantastic bargain, signing Rob Jones from Fourth Division Crewe Alexandra for a paltry £300,000. Within months, Jones would be a regular feature in the first-team and would receive his first England cap.

However, during this period, Liverpool had remained consistently inconsistent in Europe as well as domestically, defeating Finnish side Kuusysi Lahti

6-2 on aggregate – despite losing the second leg 1-0 in Finland – and coming back from 2-0 down after the first leg against French team Auxerre to win the tie 3-2, with a 3-0 victory at Anfield. A 6-0 aggregate win over FC Swarovski Tirol in December put Liverpool through to the quarter-finals to face Genoa. In the League Cup, however, Liverpool were knocked out by Third Division opposition in Peterborough United.

Following that defeat, Liverpool went on their best run of the season, going unbeaten in their next ten league matches. The first was a 1-1 draw away at The Dell against Southampton, a game most notable for featuring the first league goal of young Jamie Redknapp – one of Dalglish's last signings, for £350,000 in January 1991. Much like McManaman, Redknapp would feature heavily throughout the 1990s at Anfield. Mark Wright also returned from injury as captain and helped to strengthen the spine of Souness's team. In the week following the Southampton draw, Liverpool paid Arsenal £1.5m for midfielder Michael Thomas, the scorer of the famous last-minute goal that broke Anfield hearts in May 1989.

Thomas's signing led many on Merseyside to believe that Steve McMahon would be on his way out of Anfield. The day before, McMahon had scored the opener as Liverpool won 2-0 against Brian Clough's Nottingham Forest. On Christmas Eve, McMahon was sold to Manchester City for £900,000, and Liverpool lost a player who had been a key component of Dalglish's dominant teams. Souness would later admit that many of Dalglish's core players were unhappy with the contracts handed out to new signings Dean Saunders and Mark Wright, and McMahon was one such example. He, much like Peter Beardsley in the summer, was a casualty of Souness's haste to rebuild the team, something he would later admit was a crucial mistake during his tenure.

Despite ending December with a series of draws, including against Everton in the second Merseyside derby of the season, the Reds were now sixth in the table but still 12 points behind Manchester United. In the new year, Liverpool's form continued to improve with four straight league victories and a win in the FA Cup third round over Crewe Alexandra, featuring a hat-trick from the recently returned John Barnes, along with another goal for Steve McManaman, who continued to show flashes of brilliance with the ball at his feet. While these were not the Liverpool performances of old, central-midfielder Ray Houghton was in the conversation for the best player in the First Division at this point of the season. By the end of January, despite inconsistencies, injuries and questionable decisions with personnel, Souness had guided Liverpool back up to third, still eight points adrift but at least in the running to be numbered among the top performers in the league that season.

February would be the turning point in the club's fortunes and, unfortunately, it was a negative change rather than a positive one. Liverpool were winless in the league throughout the month, losing to Chelsea and Norwich City and drawing against Coventry City and Southampton. What's more, John Barnes, Steve Nicol and Jan Mølby picked up injuries, giving Souness further headaches relating to squad availability. Liverpool would also require a replay to progress through the fourth round of the FA Cup, drawing 1-1 with Bristol Rovers of the Second Division before winning 2-1 at Anfield. Often, Liverpool's football looked untidy and featured key individual errors. There was a growing sentiment that teams were no longer afraid to play them as they'd been in the past. February closed with Liverpool again needing a replay to defeat Second Division opposition in the FA Cup, this time Ipswich Town.

March again reflected Liverpool's deep inconsistency with wins at Anfield against West Ham United, Tottenham Hotspur and Notts County, but away defeats to Crystal Palace and Sheffield United, when they failed to get on the scoresheet. However, Liverpool defeated Aston Villa 1-0 in the FA Cup sixth round, but then crashed out of the UEFA Cup over two legs against Genoa 4-1 on aggregate, including a 2-1 defeat at Anfield.

As Liverpool headed into the final weeks of the season, realistically they were only competing in the FA Cup, with surprise semi-finalists Portsmouth their opponents at Highbury. Liverpool came through the semi-final, again needing a replay – on penalties this time – but only won once in the league all month, ironically at Anfield against title challengers Manchester United, a result that handed the title to Leeds United. However, the month would be more significant for the events surrounding Graeme Souness, his health and the FA Cup semi-final.

In April, Graeme Souness was taken to hospital for a significant operation on his heart. This would effectively end his season as Liverpool manager. While Ronnie Moran took charge of the team for the remainder of the season, Souness did an interview with *The Sun*, to be published if Liverpool won the FA Cup semi-final replay at Villa Park. The article featured Souness with his then girlfriend, the heading 'Loverpool'. The issue was that the replay had gone to penalties, therefore the story came out later than had been scheduled. As a result, it was published on 15 April 1992, the third anniversary of the Hillsborough Disaster that tragically claimed 97 lives. Liverpool fans reacted with anger at seeing not only their manager talking to *The Sun* – a newspaper that received massive criticism for how it handled and reported the Hillsborough Disaster – but doing so on such an important and sensitive day for Liverpool fans everywhere. Souness has since apologised to Liverpool fans, stating that he'd underestimated the level of feeling from the fans and insisting that there were members of the team and ex-players that maintained relationships with *The Sun*. He added that he's hurt whenever the issue is mentioned. In the eyes of many Liverpool fans, however, the matter was enough for Souness to be sacked. The issue has never really gone away and for many it was a turning point not only in Souness's time in charge, but his relationship with Liverpool Football Club.

Back in the league, Liverpool ended the season with a 0-0 draw against Sheffield Wednesday. This meant that Souness's first full season in charge at Anfield had seen the Reds falling from second the previous year to sixth. While injuries had taken their toll throughout the season, Liverpool had noticeably changed under Souness and the process would continue for the remainder of his reign. The liver bird looked to have well and truly fallen off its perch.

However, Liverpool did come away from the 1991/92 season with silverware, as they defeated Sunderland 2-0 at Wembley in the FA Cup Final. Ronnie Moran walked the team out on to the hallowed turf, but Souness had travelled to London – against the advice of his doctors – and saw McManaman dribble down the right wing to create the first goal for Michael Thomas. In a disappointing season, McManaman was certainly a bright spot. Anfield legend Ian Rush ended an injury-ravaged season by scoring the second after some nice interplay between Saunders and Thomas. Captain Mark Wright lifted the trophy for the Reds faithful who had travelled south, but, as the season ended, it was clear that things at Anfield weren't quite the same. The 1992/93 season would be the first year of the new Premier League, and Liverpool would have to do better in this brave new world of English football.

That summer saw yet more change for the playing staff at Anfield. The first surprising sale of the transfer window was that of Ray Houghton for £825,000 to Aston Villa. He'd arguably been Liverpool's best player from central midfield in 1991/92 and finished the season just behind Dean Saunders in the goalscoring charts. Houghton had undoubtedly carried the team at certain points the previous season. Also leaving Anfield was Barry Venison, who moved north to Tyneside to join Newcastle United for £250,000. However, the most shocking sale of the window was the former record signing Dean Saunders, who joined Aston Villa, along with Houghton, for £2.3m in September. Saunders – who Souness had signed for £2.9m the previous summer – was the club's top goalscorer in 1991/92 with 23 goals in all competitions, but only ten in the First Division. This was a noticeable decline from the 16 goals scored by both John Barnes and Ian Rush in 1990/91. Saunders was often asked to play a different role than the one he had at Derby County, getting more involved in build-up and being far more patient with the ball. Despite his hard work throughout the 1991/92 season, it was clear that he didn't possess the attributes required. Liverpool lost

£600,000 on the deal and the move yet again highlighted the mistake made in selling Peter Beardsley the year before to city rivals Everton.

Arriving at Anfield was goalkeeper David James, signed from Watford for £1m. With long-time keeper Bruce Grobbelaar insistent on playing for his national team Zimbabwe whenever possible, it meant that he often wouldn't be available for selection. Grobbelaar had been between the posts during the reigns of Bob Paisley, Joe Fagan and Kenny Dalglish, but the signing of James – who at that point was already an England Under-21 player – signalled the beginning of the end for Grobbelaar. However, that end would just take longer to arrive than had been intended. Souness asked Grobbelaar to take James under his wing but this doesn't appear to have worked how the manager intended. The 1990/91 season had seen Grobbelaar play 55 times, but he would only wear the jersey ten times in 1992/93.

Another arrival was Paul Stewart from Tottenham Hotspur for £2.3m. Stewart was a versatile player who had played for Tottenham for the previous four seasons, but many questioned whether he was worth the large fee. In the end, his performances in the famous red shirt would suggest otherwise. Another ill-advised signing was Torben Piechnik, who had performed well for Denmark in the latter stages of Euro 1992, demonstrating an excellent ability to man-mark opposition forwards. Unfortunately, this wouldn't translate into what he was asked to do at Liverpool. Piechnik would later join from Danish team FCK for just £500,000.

As FA Cup-winners, Liverpool's 1992/93 season began at Wembley against Leeds United in the Charity Shield, where they lost a seven-goal thriller that featured a hat-trick by the mercurial Eric Cantona, who before long would find his way to Old Trafford. Grobbelaar maintained the No. 1 shirt for now, but Paul Stewart made his debut in midfield. Leeds took the lead through Cantona in the 26th minute with a guided finish in the box, but were pegged back after a wonderful dribble and cross by Ronny Rosenthal that left Ian Rush perfectly placed to head in at the back post. Leeds retook the lead following a deflected free kick from Tony Dorigo. In the second half, Dean Saunders equalised in one of his final performances for the club, picking up a fortunate loose ball just inside the penalty area and firing home. However, Cantona then took over, making it 3-2 after a floated free kick into the area wasn't dealt with, and the Frenchman fired into the bottom corner. He then sealed his hat-trick with a header at the back post, a finish most notable for the fact that Grobbelaar had come off his line to claim the ball but got nowhere near it. A Gordon Strachan own goal made it 4-3, but, despite an afternoon of entertaining football for the neutral, there were warning signs for both teams.

Although Leeds were reigning champions, they went on to finish 17th out of the 22 teams in the Premier

League. For Liverpool, those warnings signs would prove to be omens as August ended with Souness's team having won only one league match, a 2-1 victory against Sheffield United at Anfield. Liverpool lost twice, first against Nottingham Forest – who were relegated at the end of the season – at the City Ground, and then 2-0 against Arsenal at Anfield. The Reds ended the month with consecutive 2-2 draws, first against newly promoted Ipswich Town and then Leeds United.

Young £1m signing David James was between the posts to start the Premier League season and had a difficult start. Against Forest, he saved Liverpool on several occasions before Teddy Sheringham smashed a beauty into the top corner from inside the box. James then went on to make mistakes over the month – conceding eight goals – but also showed the potential to be Liverpool's keeper for the future, including some excellent stops against Arsenal at Anfield. As Bruce Grobbelaar would often be unavailable due to matches for Zimbabwe, Souness would later explain that he didn't feel he could rely on Liverpool's long-term No. 1. Unfortunately, this did little for immediate results, as Liverpool ended the month of August in a lowly 16th place with only five points from five matches.

September yielded more misery at Anfield. Barnes, Mølby, Thomas, Stewart and Whelan spent time on the injury list and Liverpool again won only once in the Premier League all month. They started with a 1-1 draw against Southampton at Anfield after a Mark Wright header levelled a Le Tissier-created opener for the Hampshire club. Staying at Anfield, Liverpool then won their only league match of the month, against Chelsea, with goals from Saunders – his last for the club – and Jamie Redknapp. Redknapp's goal was a sliding finish at the back post that gave Liverpool the win in the 89th minute. However, this was followed by a 1-0 away defeat to Sheffield United before Liverpool travelled to face Aston Villa at Villa Park. By this point, Villa's starting line-up featured three former Liverpool players in Dean Saunders, Ray Houghton and Steve Staunton. In a match that was perhaps a statement about Liverpool's decision-making over the previous year and a half, Aston Villa won 4-2, with Saunders scoring a brace, the second assisted by Houghton. This match also saw the debut of Torben Piechnik in a Liverpool shirt. The man he marked was Dean Saunders.

Liverpool closed out September with a 3-2 defeat to Wimbledon as they dropped to an unbelievable 19th place. Prior to the match, David James had been awarded the Young Eagle of the Month Award, but it was Bruce Grobbelaar who returned in goal after James had let in four – including a howler from a pass-back – against Third Division Chesterfield in the League Cup. James wouldn't regain his place until January. Liverpool had at least won in the European Cup Winners' Cup, 8-2 on aggregate against Cypriot team Apollon Limassol.

Liverpool's form did improve through October and November, losing only once in the league, a 2-0 defeat to Tottenham at White Hart Lane. The Reds won against Sheffield Wednesday, Middlesbrough, Queens Park Rangers and Crystal Palace. They also had a victory against surprise contenders Norwich City. Perhaps most impressively, though, Liverpool went to Old Trafford to face Manchester United – who were once again in the title picture – going two up before half-time through Rush and the in-form Don Hutchison. Hutchison would go on to make 42 appearances in the 1992/93 season and score ten goals but had the reputation of being a physical player, despite being a capable passer. Unfortunately, Manchester United came back after half-time through Mark Hughes in the 78th and 90th minutes, but it was a strong sign that Liverpool's form had recovered.

By the end of November, the Reds were up to eighth in the table. However, while their fortunes appeared to be looking up in the league, they'd crashed out of the Cup Winners' Cup in the second round against Russian team Spartak Moscow, losing 6-2 on aggregate, including a disappointing 2-0 loss at Anfield. Of note in the away leg, however, was a horrendous error by Grobbelaar, who mis-controlled the ball on the edge of his box, playing it directly into the path of Valeri Karpin who made it 2-1. Liverpool did progress in the League Cup, but required a replay against Sheffield United. During this period, Ian Rush also score his 200th league goal for Liverpool, despite his dry spell during the first half of the season. At the end of November, John Barnes also returned for the first time since September.

However, everything came crashing down over the Christmas period as Liverpool managed only two league victories throughout December and January, with a collective record of two wins, four losses and one draw, causing them to fall out of the top half of the table, ending January down in 12th. During this run, they lost against Wimbledon, Aston Villa – with Saunders scoring again – Coventry City and, most disappointingly, in the Merseyside derby at Goodison Park against Everton. Liverpool actually went 1-0 up through Mark Wright's header from a corner, but were quickly pegged back by Mo Johnstone, a player who had been linked with Liverpool early in Souness's reign. In the end, Everton scored the winner five minutes from time, as former Liverpool star Peter Beardsley marked possibly his greatest moment in an Everton shirt with a guided finish into the bottom corner from the edge of the box.

Most infuriatingly for those on the red half of Merseyside, it still felt as if Liverpool were trying to replace the quality Beardsley had provided, over a year and a half after he'd left Anfield. Souness decided to re-enter the transfer market at the beginning of December, signing Stig Inge Bjørnebye for £600,000 from Norwegian club Rosenborg. Intended as a replacement for left-back David Burrows, Bjørnebye would struggle to adapt to the Premier League and returned to Norway on loan in 1994, before eventually becoming a much-loved part of the Reds team of the 1990s.

December also featured disappointment in the League Cup, as the Reds were knocked out after a 2-1 replay defeat to Crystal Palace. January then saw them crash out of the FA Cup in the fourth round against Bolton Wanderers, with the Second Division team winning a replay 2-0 at Anfield. After two full seasons with Souness in the Anfield dugout, it was noticeable how often Liverpool required replays to progress in the cup competitions. This often meant that rotation was essential and it put pressure on a squad that had suffered badly from injuries to key players.

Liverpool then went winless in February, drawing against Nottingham Forest, Chelsea, Ipswich Town and Sheffield Wednesday, and losing 2-1 at The Dell against Southampton. Souness made a bold statement against Wednesday, dropping Ian Rush from the line-up. Rush had undoubtedly had a poor season up to this point but Liverpool were hardly prolific as a team, scoring only twice in the entire month, both times through Don Hutchison. March then began with a 2-1 defeat at Anfield against Manchester United, with Rush finally getting back on the scoresheet. The defeat saw Liverpool fall to 15th, a mere three points above the drop zone. Relegation was a legitimate possibility. With

Manchester United top of the table – and about to go on an unbeaten run to seal the inaugural Premier League title – it was hard not to make the comparison between the two clubs. Liverpool had declined in quality, were no longer the dominant team in English football and were unrecognisable from the best teams of Dalglish's era.

Fortunately for the Anfield faithful, March saw Liverpool's recovery begin, although it also featured Bruce Grobbelaar going on loan to Second Division Stoke City for the remainder of the season. Liverpool went unbeaten for the remainder of the month, with wins against Queens Park Rangers, Middlesbrough and in the second derby of the season against Everton. The catalyst for this turnaround was the return to form of Ian Rush, who ended the month with four goals in five matches as the Reds moved away from the relegation zone and up to tenth in the table. Rush would go on to finish the season with 22 goals in all competitions.

As April began, he also scored against Kenny Dalglish's Blackburn Rovers at Ewood Park. Unfortunately, Rush's goal came in the 84th minute after a dominant performance by Dalglish's team saw Liverpool 4-0 down. Blackburn would go on to finish fourth in the league, 12 points ahead of Souness's team. Dalglish had joined Blackburn while they were in the Second Division, and this was yet another clear statement about where Liverpool now stood in comparison to the rest of the league. Despite the defeat, they did continue their good form through the remainder of April, with Anfield being treated to wins against Oldham Athletic, Coventry City and Leeds United. The Oldham match saw one of Rush's best goals of the season, as he picked the ball up on the right flank and cut inside before smashing the ball into the top corner with his weaker foot from around 20 yards. Mark Walters netted a hattrick against Coventry, his best performance in some time in the famous red shirt. As the month ended, Liverpool had quite amazingly jumped up to fifth in the table. Only ten points would eventually separate sixth from 20th.

Liverpool's disappointing 1992/93 season ended with two away defeats, against Norwich City and Oldham, before closing out with a 6-2 demolition of Tottenham, with Rush, Barnes and Walters all scoring in the final ten minutes to send the Anfield crowd home happy for the summer. Liverpool's final league position was sixth for a second consecutive season; however, this season had progressed differently from 1991/92, with only a late run of good form inspired by Ian Rush dragging the club back up the table to a position that would be considered respectable. There was a significant gap between Liverpool in sixth up to the top four of Manchester United, Aston Villa, Norwich City and Blackburn Rovers, and had Rush not hit form in March, the Reds could easily have finished in the bottom half of the table.

The 1991/92 campaign had at least seen the breakthrough of Steve McManaman into the first team, and while Jamie Redknapp had received playing time in midfield, McManaman in particular hadn't developed in the same way that fellow young winger Ryan Giggs had at Manchester United. That year, Giggs won the PFA Young Player of the Year award, while McManaman wasn't in the top three, having finished second the previous year.

Throughout the season, calls for Souness to be sacked had grown louder and louder, and it had become clear that the team had declined in quality and that a significant improvement would certainly be needed in 1993/94. However, the concern for many on Merseyside was that, since taking over, many of Souness's decisions could be said to be questionable at the very least. Souness himself would later state that some of his signings hadn't been as good as he had wanted them to be, but he considered the team to be better than when he took over and it was a young team that would only improve, rather than an older team that would decline. While changes were needed at the end of Dalglish's tenure, this was definitely an optimistic assessment from Souness. In reality, Liverpool were now undoubtedly on the wane, with a much weaker squad, featuring players that many felt simply weren't up to the standard required to play at the club.

Souness overhauled the squad further during the summer of 1993. Leaving the club was Mike Hooper, who had started in goal for much of the previous season when Bruce Grobbelaar was unavailable, while David James had been dropped. Hooper joined Kevin Keegan's newly promoted Newcastle United for £550,000. Under Keegan, Newcastle would take the Premier League by storm in 1993/94, finishing third while playing a brand of football that was loved by neutrals across the country. Also leaving Anfield was Hungarian István Kozma, who had been signed in February 1992 from Dunfermline but never looked even remotely close to making the first-team. Kozma was released on a free transfer to return to Hungary with Újpest. Further changes included the swap deal of David Burrows and Mike Marsh to West Ham United in exchange for Julian Dicks. Dicks had a reputation for being a rough player with a poor disciplinary record, having been sent off three times in 1992/93 in the First Division, thus missing a considerable amount of playing time while suspended. Weeks before signing for Liverpool, he'd severely injured new West Ham signing Simon Webster, breaking his leg. This was a clear effort by Souness to toughen up his Liverpool team, and Dicks would later say that Souness had told him that he was 'his kind of player' and that he didn't want him to change his style of play. Also joining that summer was defender Neil Ruddock, who came in for £2.5m from Tottenham Hotspur. Ruddock was also perceived as a 'hard man' by fans and would feature for Liverpool throughout the 90s. Souness felt that Dicks and Ruddock were better players than they received credit for, but for many on Merseyside, it appeared as though Souness was taking the club further away from its passing, attacking ethos and towards a physical style of play. Uncertainty grew around Anfield.

Souness's first signing of the summer had actually been another attempt to replace the giant Peter Beardsley-shaped hole next to Ian Rush. At this point, Beardsley was joining Newcastle for £1.5m and was about to have a fantastic comeback season, supplying goals for Andy Cole, who would top the goalscoring charts with 34 league goals. Souness decided to sign Nigel Clough from relegated Nottingham Forest for £2.28m. Clough had scored ten league goals for Forest in 1992/93, with him and Roy Keane being their only reliable players of quality that year. Unlike Dicks, Clough possessed many of the qualities valued in a Liverpool player, meaning in this case, creativity and composure in possession. He would also be handed the famous No. 7 shirt worn by Keegan, Dalglish and Beardsley. On the pitch, despite a positive start, things would never really click for Clough at Anfield, and his signing would turn out to be yet another example of Souness failing to fill the gaps that he himself had created in his haste to rebuild the squad once he took over.

The 1993/94 Premier League season began brilliantly for Souness's team, as they opened up with four victories in five matches. In front of over 40,000 at Anfield, Nigel

Clough marked his debut with a brace, guiding the ball into the top corner from the right-hand side of the box for his first and scoring a simple tap-in for his second as Liverpool won 2-0 against Sheffield Wednesday. Liverpool's line-up that day demonstrated the changes that Souness had brought to the club. The starting XI was Grobbelaar, Jones, Nicol, Wright, Bjørnebye, Ruddock, Clough, Walters, Whelan, Mølby and Rush. Of the starters, only six had been at the club in 1991. The Reds followed their opening-day victory with an entertaining 3-1 away win in London against Queens Park Rangers, as Ian Rush scored his first of the season and Clough scored his third. Souness's team then travelled to newly promoted Swindon Town and demolished them 5-0, with Ruddock, Whelan, Marsh and McManaman on the scoresheet, the latter scoring twice in his best performance in a Liverpool shirt for some time. The Reds were brought back down to earth with a 2-1 loss at home to Tottenham, despite a wonderfully created goal by McManaman, who found himself trapped in the corner only to execute a stunning double drag-back, and dribble down the byline, after which he cut the ball back for Clough to finish. However, Teddy Sheringham scored twice to give Tottenham the three points, but then Liverpool went on to beat Leeds United three days later at Anfield. It was hard not to notice the excellent start they'd made, ending August second in the league, one point behind Manchester United.

Unfortunately, as so many times under Souness, that good form would prove to be unsustainable, with four straight league defeats, to Coventry City, Blackburn Rovers, Chelsea and Everton in the first Merseyside derby of 1993/94, at Goodison Park. The derby was Julian Dicks's first match in the red shirt, but Bruce Grobbelaar grabbed the headlines, as he responded to a poor Steve McManaman clearance that created an Everton chance by giving the young midfielder a verbal dressing-down in front of the entire team, before pushing him away by his face. McManaman fired back, hitting the Zimbabwean in the face, but it was Grobbelaar's reaction that had caused the incident. His position had already been threatened the previous season by the signing of David James and it was becoming clearer that his time at the club was coming to an end. The incident went on to be one of the more memorable bust ups between team-mates in Premier League history. Everton's second goal in their 2-0 win was to to be a catalogue of errors from the Liverpool defence, who were unable to take control of the ball, with Tony Cottee somehow evading Julian Dicks, Mark Wright and Bruce Grobbelaar to stab the ball into the back of the net from six yards out.

The month's shocking results saw Liverpool drop from second to 13th in the table and, all of a sudden, it felt like déjà vu on Merseyside. The lone bright spot of the month was the first-team debut of 18-year old centre-forward Robbie Fowler in the League Cup, showing flashes of a developing partnership with Ian Rush and playing a part in Liverpool's first two goals, before scoring the third in a 3-1 win against Fulham in the first leg. Fowler's goal demonstrated the young Liverpudlian's goalscoring instinct, gas he got on the end of a Don Hutchison cross to half-volley the ball into the net and cap off a fantastic debut. He would go on to score plenty more throughout the 90s. Also of note was Fulham's goal, a lobbed finish by substitute Sean Farrell, with Grobbelaar caught off his line. Of course, the attention deservedly went to Robbie Fowler.

Fowler then made his first league start on 2 October in a 0-0 draw at home against Arsenal, as Liverpool at least broke their losing streak in the league, but he then followed that match with a five-goal haul in the second leg against Fulham in a 5-0 victory at Anfield. He scored with his left foot, right foot and head in a complete performance. Much like the breakthrough of McManaman had been in 1991/92, Robbie Fowler was quickly becoming the story of 1993/94. He frequently received comparisons to Ian Rush for his composure in front of goal and the ease with which he found himself in the best positions to score. This ability would never leave Fowler throughout his career, and he went on to score his first league goal in the next match, a 2-1 comeback victory against Oldham Athletic, following a missed punch by Bruce Grobbelaar that had given Oldham the lead.

Liverpool would also be forced to make a comeback in the next match, but in this game were only able to draw 1-1 against Manchester City with a late goal by Ian Rush. Fowler was back on the scoresheet against Southampton, this time scoring his first league hat-trick as Anfield witnessed a 4-2 victory. His first was a glancing header into the far corner from a Rob Jones cross, his second a wonderful control and finish from a Ruddock long ball, and the third a quickly taken free kick that Ian Rush completely missed in the penalty box and that ended up in the far corner. Rush clearly had no desire to claim the goal, running straight over to congratulate Fowler on his hat-trick. However, three days previously, Rush had scored a hat-trick of his own against Ipswich Town in the League Cup, in a 3-2 win. In the Premier League, Liverpool were up to seventh as October ended but were a massive 14 points behind Manchester United.

The Reds only played three times in November, all in the Premier League, with two victories and one defeat continuing the club's good form. They comfortably defeated West Ham United 2-0 at Anfield, with Nigel Clough scoring a rare goal in a Liverpool shirt. Robbie Fowler was again on the scoresheet in a 2-1 home victory against Aston Villa. However, the week before, on 21 November, Souness's side travelled to Tyneside to face Keegan's Newcastle United, where a prolific Andy Cole scored a first-half hat-trick as the newly promoted

Newcastle eased to a 3-0 victory, with Liverpool never really threatening.

The Reds ended November in ninth, looking more and more like a mid-table team. Again calls for Souness to be replaced grew louder and louder on Merseyside. Those calls weren't eased by their form during December, as they won only once all month, 3-2 against Queens Park Rangers at Anfield, drawing against newly promoted Swindon Town, and against Tottenham Hotspur, Sheffield United and Wimbledon. To start that month, Liverpool lost 3-1 away to Sheffield Wednesday, with Wednesday's third goal being down to another error by Bruce Grobbelaar as the keeper came way out of his box and completely missed the ball, leading to an easy tap-in for Mark Bright. Grobbelaar also handed QPR their opening goal in the next match, playing the ball directly to Les Ferdinand as he tried to clear his lines. December also saw the Reds knocked out of the League Cup in the fourth round, losing a replay on penalties to Wimbledon at Selhurst Park. As 1993 turned to 1994, Liverpool were in eighth place. Manchester United remained top of the table, 23 points ahead of the Anfield club. The improvement that Souness so badly needed in 1993/94 wasn't happening, and the pressure was growing.

Liverpool would begin the new year with an uneasy 2-1 victory away at Ipswich Town's Portman Road, Ian Rush's 88th-minute tap-in giving them the points. Souness's team then hosted reigning champions and league leaders Manchester United at Anfield. The match was one of the few from 1993/94 that Liverpool fans maintain fond memories of. Steve Bruce gave United the lead in the ninth minute with a powerful header from a floated cross by Eric Cantona. Earlier, Robbie Fowler had been through on goal against Schmeichel but fired over the bar to the disappointment of the Kop. Ryan Giggs doubled United's lead in the 20th minute, lobbing the ball over Bruce Grobbelaar into the far corner. Grobbelaar was probably too far out of his goal, but it was an impressive finish from Giggs nonetheless. Amazingly, Dennis Irwin then gave United a three-goal lead in the 24th minute, curling a free kick into the top corner from 25 yards, with Grobbelaar rooted to the spot.

However, Liverpool kept fighting and immediately posted a reply, Nigel Clough marking the high point of a difficult season by smashing the ball into the bottom corner from distance. Almost immediately, the Kop came alive and the noise around Anfield grew and grew. Clough scored his second in the 38th minute, the ball falling to him fortunately on the edge of the box, leaving him through one-on-one against Schmeichel. He tucked the ball into the corner to make it 3-2 to United. Liverpool rode their luck and threw men forward in search of an equaliser, thankful to Grobbelaar in the second half when he saved from Giggs. Schmeichel did the same for United, keeping out a curling shot from Jamie Redknapp that looked to just be sneaking in the corner. But it was Neil Ruddock who finally brought Liverpool level in the 79th minute, heading in from a Bjørnebye cross. The 3-3 draw was easily the best moment of a poor season at Anfield, but things would get worse before they got better.

In the FA Cup, Liverpool drew First Division Bristol City. Ian Rush gave Liverpool the lead before Bristol went level before half-time. Bruce Grobbelaar provided an extremely erratic first-half performance, almost gifting Bristol two goals. Perhaps luckily for Souness's team, an electrical failure at the ground saw the floodlights fail during the second half and the match was abandoned, to be played later in the month. Liverpool's next fixture was a 3-0 victory against Oldham Athletic in the league. Dicks, Fowler and Redknapp scored the goals in an easy victory. Then on 19 January Liverpool travelled back to Bristol to replay the FA Cup third-round tie. As was so often the case in previous seasons, they would trip up in the cup, drawing 1-1, so would require a replay at Anfield. To make matters worse, Robbie Fowler broke his ankle, so the young star would be out for seven weeks.

Back in the Premier League, Liverpool had Ian Rush to thank for a 2-1 comeback victory against Manchester City at Anfield, Rushie scoring both, including one in time added on. Liverpool's final match of January was the FA Cup third-round replay against Bristol City. Souness selected a strong line-up of Grobbelaar, Jones, Nicol, Harkness, Ruddock, Clough, Barnes, Walters,

Redknapp, McManaman and Rush. On the bench were James, Bjørnebye and Hutchison. Liverpool looked hesitant at the back early on and could have been 2-0 down within minutes had Bristol City's finishing been better. The home team should then have gone 1-0 up, with John Barnes through on goal, but the England international scuffed his shot wide. Liverpool had some good moments, but Bristol looked equally likely to break the deadlock, and probably should have when dangerous keeping from Grobbelaar left Liam Robinson with an open goal from about 25 yards, but the forward put his shot just over the bar.

As the second half began, Bristol City continued to defend well – if admittedly riding their luck at times. Souness brought Don Hutchison on for Jamie Redknapp. Despite being a regular in 1992/93, Hutchison had found appearances harder to come by this season and this was one of only 15 appearances for the club in 1993/94. Bristol City changed tactics for the second half, moving Brian Tinnion from the left wing to sit behind the strikers. The decision had been made prior to the game due to Liverpool's preference for the 4-4-2 system, but manager Russell Osman deliberately waited until after half-time to make the switch.

Liverpool continued to press forward and nearly took the lead when Rush slid in to get his foot on a McManaman cross, but the ball went just over the bar. However, with Tinnion controlling play from an

TIME GOES BY – LIVERPOOL UNDER SOUNESS

attacking midfield position, Bristol started to move the ball more effectively in the middle of the park, and they should have taken the lead when Junior Bent fired over the bar when it seemed easier to score, the ball falling to him unmarked in the penalty box. In the 66th minute, Bristol cleared the ball from a goal kick and the ball was nodded forward. It was then hooked on by Liam Robinson and fell to Tinnion after a poor header by Neil Ruddock. Tinnion then played the ball to Wayne Allison, who tried to go for goal himself, but as he was tackled by Rob Jones, the ball fell into the path of Tinnion, who had continued his run. With a sweep of his left foot the ball nestled in the bottom corner. Bristol City were 1-0 up at Anfield. Liverpool pushed forward again but should have conceded another before the end of match and never really looked like equalising. As the final whistle went and Bristol City celebrated a memorable cup upset, boos and whistles went around Anfield in anger and disgust, as fans realised that, effectively, Liverpool's season was over. Once again, calls for Souness to be sacked returned.

Just 48 hours later, Graeme Souness resigned as manager of Liverpool Football Club after a 33-month spell in charge. In his statement, he admitted that he'd found the job tougher than he'd expected. He said that injuries had taken a toll on the squad and had forced him to bring young players into the squad quicker than would usually be expected at Anfield, and that parting ways was the best thing for himself and for the club. While he was correct that injuries had affected the squad over the past two seasons, the mistakes were clear to see. Too much was changed too quickly, leaving significant gaps in quality that Souness was unable to fill throughout his tenure. Peter Beardsley is just one example, but it was clear throughout the entirety of his reign as manager that Souness was looking to find a strike partner for Ian Rush, while Beardsley continued to be a Premier League-level player throughout this period.

When Souness took over, it was clear that changes did need to be made to the squad, but there was no reason for Liverpool to fall off their perch quite so severely as they had through his management. Souness angered experienced players by handing out larger contracts to new signings, when the experienced players were the ones that had kept Dalglish's Liverpool at the very top of English football. Souness also repeatedly failed in the transfer market. Dean Saunders, Paul Stewart, Torben Piechnik, Nigel Clough, Paul Dicks and Michael Thomas were all signings that failed at Anfield under Souness, and many others, such as David James, would take time to recover. Souness might have said that he was forced to bring young players in, but he arguably held back the development of Steve McManaman by signing players that could play in the same position as he did.

The Liverpool job might have been more difficult than he'd expected but it's an inescapable fact that, under Souness, Liverpool declined from being a top club in English football to one that faced battles just to compete for European places. Sir Alex Ferguson might have famously claimed to want to 'knock Liverpool off their perch', but it was the decisions that Liverpool – and therefore Souness – made from 1991 to 1994 that contributed just as much to the changing of the guard in English football. After 33 months, Graeme Souness was leaving Liverpool and his relationship with the club has never been quite the same.

The then Liverpool chairman David Moores stated that the club intended to appoint a new manager quickly, but that no announcement could yet be made. The anticipated replacement within the media was Roy Evans, Souness's assistant manager and long-term boot-room member. Also leaving Anfield in January 1994 was Ronny Rosenthal, who joined Tottenham for £250,000. He'd featured regularly under Souness but, like Liverpool as a team, he remained consistently inconsistent and so often flattered to deceive. Whoever took over as manager, things would have to change.

Chapter 2

Move Over – Return of the Boot Room

WITH GRAEME Souness departing Anfield, the search was now on for a new manager for the dugout. Whoever Liverpool chairman David Moores appointed to the post full time, it was clear that this would be a defining moment in the history of Liverpool Football Club. Under Souness, they'd declined towards mid-table and, if the board were to get this appointment wrong, Liverpool could easily follow the same pattern as previous great teams that slid towards mid-table mediocrity. For many, the favourite for the job was Roy Evans, a loyal assistant manager to Souness and a long-term coach and member of the legendary boot room. If Evans was appointed as manager, it would signal a return to the old policy of promoting from within that the club had abandoned when enlisting Souness as manager in April 1991.

By January 1994 Evans had been a part of the Liverpool set-up for around 30 years. He played for England Schoolboys before becoming a professional Liverpool player in October 1965. He was born in Bootle on Merseyside, an area that suffered throughout the 1960s and 1970s as industrial decline severely impacted the city of Liverpool and the surrounding area of Merseyside. As a player, Evans found appearances in the legendary Bill Shankly's team hard to come by, during a time when Shankly was rebuilding his first great team into his second great one, which would hit a peak under the stewardship of Bob Paisley. Evans made three appearances in the 1969/70 First Division, and four in 1970/71, but struggled to get into the team as Liverpool won the First Division in 1972/73 by three points from Arsenal. In total, Roy Evans made only nine appearances for the first team, but eventually he moved into coaching in his mid-twenties after Shankly offered him a place on the staff. Evans later admitted that he didn't want to be a coach but it was clear that he wasn't going to get in the team as a player after years of trying, and he had no desire to leave Liverpool.

Evans joined the group of coaches that formed the legendary boot room that drove the on-field direction of Liverpool Football Club during its dominant period during the 70s and 80s. The boot room – literally just a room full of boots located in the bowels of Anfield – was a place where the coaching staff informally discussed issues with the team – often with beer or whisky as light refreshment. It was the place where in 1973 Shankly met with Joe Fagan, Bob Paisley, Ronnie Moran, Tom Saunders, and Reuben Bennett, and came to the conclusion that the reason Red Star Belgrade had beaten them 4-2 on aggregate in the second round of the European Cup was the ability of the Yugoslav team to keep possession and be patient with the ball. A decision was then made that Liverpool should strive for this style of play, building from the back and playing patient football. It saw classic stopper centre-backs such as Larry Lloyd replaced with more technically gifted players such as Phil Thompson, and culminated in the introduction of Alan Hansen, the most elegant British defender of his generation. In short, this was 'the Liverpool Way', and it was these traditions that Roy Evans had been educated in.

As well as working with the first team, Paisley – now manager following Shankly's retirement – also put Evans in charge of the reserve team, a unit he knew well from his playing days. Evans ran the team in his own way, playing a style of football that was becoming synonymous with Liverpool, but he had the freedom to pick whichever players he wanted. Evans's Liverpool reserves regularly won their league. Whenever the reserves weren't playing, Evans listened to Moran and Fagan with the first team and clearing up as much as he could. He also worked as a physio, soaking up injuries with the use of the much-celebrated magic sponge. He would later talk about the collaborative approach within the boot room, that meant coaches were able to give their own opinions on team matters, with an understanding that, once the manager had made a decision, it was never questioned or undermined. This perhaps explains why Evans didn't have as much of an impact during Souness's tenure as many on Merseyside may have liked.

Whoever came in and took on the job of helping Liverpool recover, it wouldn't be an easy task. The club's famed style of play had gradually eroded over the past two and a half seasons, with more physical players such as Dicks and Ruddock being brought in. Furthermore, young players had either come into the club or emerged through the youth set-up and needed help to develop. Steve McManaman showed utter brilliance in flashes, Jamie Redknapp possessed excellent control and passing in the middle of the park but needed work on his defensive game, and Robbie Fowler simply needed nurturing into the player who would take over from Rush as Liverpool's star striker. The Reds had also signed the promising young David James the season before, but his Anfield career had been inconsistent thus far, with the former England Under-21 goalkeeper in and out of the team, and in and out of form as a result. Most importantly, the team needed a boost in confidence. Their form had never been consistent during Souness's reign and it was clear that confidence continued to be an issue. After the Bristol City defeat, Jamie Redknapp described it as the lowest point of his career. As a football club and a family, Liverpool had lost their way and needed someone to come in to bring the spirit back.

In the end, the board decided that Roy Evans was the man for the job. Chairman David Moores rang him and invited him to his house. Evans would later admit that he wasn't sure whether he was going to be offered the job or told his services at the club would no longer be required, but much to his delight it was the former. With little interest for his own monetary gain, Roy Evans accepted the job and on 31 January 1994 officially became the 14th manager in the great history of Liverpool Football Club. On the journey home, he wondered what he was getting into but he reasoned that he knew the club, what the job entailed and had the support of a fantastic coaching staff in Ronnie Moran, Doug Livermore, Sammy Lee and Chris Lawler. Using Joe Fagan's approach as a template, he took over a Liverpool team that sat fifth in the table but with nothing to play for over the remainder of the 1993/94 season. Evans reassured the fans, saying things certainly weren't as bad at the club as many seemed to believe, but had he aimed to restore it to its rightful place in English football.

That same month, Phil Boersma, who had been with Souness at Rangers and followed him to Liverpool, left the club, eventually joining back up with Souness at Turkish club Galatasaray. The Souness era was over at Anfield and the boot room had returned to prominence, but the hard work for Evans and the coaching staff had just begun. The first job was finishing the 1993/94 season and evaluating the squad that Souness had left behind.

Chapter 3

Spice – Ending the 93/94 Season

AS JANUARY 1994 ended and February began, new Liverpool manager Roy Evans got to work. Change was certainly needed on Merseyside, with many of Graeme Souness's signings either lacking the required quality to play in the red shirt of Liverpool or lacking the right mentality to play in 'the Liverpool Way'. Nevertheless, with little for the Reds to play for in the Premier League – as Manchester United romped to a second straight league title – and having been knocked out of both major cup competitions, the rest of the season would serve as a period of grace for the new manager, when he assessed the squad's strengths and weaknesses. It would also help Evans to plan out future recruitment and identify where the club's money would best be utilised in the transfer market.

However, again things were about to get worse before they got better, as the ending of the season wasn't a pretty one in terms of results.

Evans's Liverpool tenure began away from home at Carrow Road against Norwich City, who had flown high the year before – top in the early portion of the season – to eventually finish third, but this season found the Canaries languishing in mid-table. The first team selection that Roy Evans made as Liverpool boss was Grobbelaar, Jones, Dicks, Wright, Clough, Barnes, Walters, Whelan, McManaman, Matteo and Rush. David James, Torben Piechnik and Don Hutchison made up the bench. Most notable from Evans's first line-up was the selection of Ronnie Whelan, a Liverpool legend who had suffered under the management of Souness, losing the captaincy and his No. 5 shirt upon the arrival of Mark Wright. Whelan's appearance against Norwich was his first league start since the Merseyside derby in September.

Against Norwich, Liverpool went 1-0 down early on after a scruffy Chris Sutton goal in the 12th minute, but they pegged the Canaries back after half-time when some nice passing from Whelan found Rush in the channel, whose cross led to an own goal by Ian Culverhouse. Sutton made it 2-1 ten minutes later, however, with a wonderful curving shot from 20 yards that gave Grobbelaar absolutely no chance. Liverpool then drew level again before full time, Julian Dicks lofting a pass into the area, leading to John Barnes tucking the ball into the bottom corner after a scuffle that saw Rush make considerable contact with the Norwich keeper,

Bryan Gunn. In the modern game, VAR would surely overturn the goal, but it stood and Liverpool came away from East Anglia with a hard-earned draw. Barnes celebrated scoring with Rush and Whelan, walking away from goal clenching his fist. Much like Whelan, Barnes had suffered under Souness, being criticised for a lack of fitness and questioned about whether he was the same player he'd been in the late-80s. Barnes might have been a different player from when he was at his peak but he remained important at Anfield and the coming years would see the England international change and adapt his game to match Evans's demands.

However, February then took a turn for the worse for the Reds, as they lost two straight. The first was in the snow at The Dell, 4-2 to Southampton, thanks to a hat-trick by the phenomenal Matt Le Tissier. Liverpool scored through Julian Dicks from the penalty spot and Ian Rush to keep the scoreline at least respectable, but Southampton were comfortable winners in the end. Five days later, Evans's team travelled to Elland Road to face Howard Wilkinson's Leeds United and were beaten 2-0. The defeat would be the final appearance of Bruce Grobbelaar as Liverpool goalkeeper. He came out to claim a Gary McAllister cross but ended up merely flapping at the ball, allowing David Wetherall to tuck it into the bottom corner. Grobbelaar had always had these mistakes in his locker – in fact, it was part of his charm as a goalkeeper – but the excellent stop-stopping that had always come with it had declined, and these mistakes had become more frequent in the Souness era. Grobbelaar went off injured late in the match, with David James replacing him between the posts. It was over the next several weeks that Evans decided to make the switch in goal. David James would go on to be Liverpool's No. 1 for the next few years.

Back at Anfield, Liverpool at least closed out a difficult February with a win over Coventry City, with Ian Rush getting an early goal that kept them fifth in the table. Rush's goal was a lovely finish after some excellent work by Redknapp and McManaman to set up the legendary striker. McManaman later hit the post, once more showing flashes of his clear potential.

March again proved to be an inconsistent month for the Reds – a problem still hanging over from Souness's reign – with two wins and three defeats in the Premier League. Kenny Dalglish's Blackburn Rovers were up first and comfortably eased past Liverpool 2-0 through Jason Wilcox and Tim Sherwood. Although Manchester United would go on to win their second straight league title, it was clear that Blackburn were a team with a lot of momentum, representing a dichotomy between the clubs. Next for Liverpool came the second Merseyside derby of the season, the Reds having lost the first encounter in a match remembered for Bruce Grobbelaar's altercation with Steve McManaman. There was less drama in the Anfield fixture, which saw the return of Robbie Fowler from his broken ankle sustained against Bristol City in January.

Everton went 1-0 up in the 20th minute, centre-back Dave Watson heading in from a free kick that was foolishly given away by Julian Dicks just outside the penalty area. Liverpool were bailed out instantly – as so often throughout their history – by Ian Rush, who finished off a Dicks long ball to make it 1-1 as the Kop exploded. The Reds then went close through Steve McManaman, who had his shot saved from 20 yards, but they took the lead when John Barnes came infield and nudged the ball forward for Robbie Fowler, who beat the offside trap and tucked the ball away into the bottom corner as if he'd never been away. Fowler celebrated with Rush, the ecstasy of the moment clear to see from the look on his face. Liverpool continued to push in the second half and almost scored through Rush and McManaman – who once again was showing his class – but the match end 2-1, easily one of Liverpool's better performances that season, and the best of Evans's reign thus far. The victory was secured by David James, who saved a last-minute shot by Peter Beagrie that looked to be going in the corner following a heavy deflection. It was a big moment for James as he continued to keep Bruce Grobbelaar out of the starting line-up.

Liverpool's next match was also at Anfield, this time hosting Chelsea. The Reds again won 2-1, taking the lead through Rush after a nice cross from Fowler created a tap-in for the club captain. Their second ended up being given as an own goal by Craig Burley, but in reality either John Barnes or Robbie Fowler could have scored the header after some excellent work on the right wing by Steve McManaman, who was fantastic again when Liverpool travelled to Highbury to face Arsenal, but Evans's team came away from London with a 1-0 defeat after a goal by Paul Merson. Liverpool's last match of March saw them travel away from Anfield again, this time to league leaders Manchester United at Old Trafford. Despite attacking relentlessly and having a definite penalty turned down by the officials, a Paul Ince header gave the champions elect a 1-0 victory. As March ended, Liverpool fell to sixth.

April and May proved to be difficult as Liverpool headed towards the end of the Premier League season. They began April with a disappointing 2-1 loss at Anfield against Sheffield United, who would eventually be relegated. Ian Rush opened the scoring in the first five minutes, before Jostein Flo scored twice, both goals featuring poor defending on Liverpool's part. Two days later, the Reds drew 1-1 with Joe Kinnear's in-form Wimbledon team at a muddy Selhurst Park. In the end, the poor playing surface helped give Liverpool the lead, with Jamie Redknapp's shot from 20 yards bobbling over Hans Segers as the keeper dived to his right. They held on until added time, when they were extremely unfortunate as a deflected free kick from Gary Elkins completely wrong-footed David James and nestled in the back of the net. Liverpool dropped to seventh.

Back at Anfield, Liverpool picked up their penultimate win of the season, a late Dicks penalty against Ipswich keeping the Reds seventh. The penalty was won by Don Hutchison in one of his final appearances for the club. The next side to visit Anfield were Kevin Keegan's superb Newcastle United, at this point far above Liverpool, up in third and playing a wonderful brand of attacking football. Keegan's team came away from Anfield with a relatively easy 2-0 win through Robert Lee and Andy Cole, who would go on to win the PFA Young Player of the Year award. Liverpool's final success of the season was against West Ham United, winning 2-1 away at the Boleyn Ground through Fowler and Rush.

They then lost their final two league matches of the season, 1-0 against Norwich City and 2-1 against Aston Villa – with Fowler scoring his 12th league goal of the season – but the most significant moment at the end of Liverpool's 1993/94 season was the final day of standing on the Kop on 30 April 1994. Due to recommendations in the Taylor Report conducted following the Hillsborough Disaster regarding safety at football stadiums, the all-standing Kop was to undergo reconstruction over the summer, to be converted into an all-seater stand that remains at Anfield to this day. Liverpool might have played Norwich City that day, but for many who were present – including Billy Liddell, Tommy Smith, Phil Thompson, Kenny Dalglish, Joe Fagan, Jessie Paisley and Nessie Shankly – the main attraction was saying goodbye to an institution of Liverpool Football Club. Banners filled the legendary stand as the club said its farewells to one final rendition of 'You'll Never Walk Alone'. Evans stated that he and his coaching staff were disappointed in the team's performance that day but that it was clear the fans hadn't let it affect a special day for the club.

So, after a tumultuous 1993/94 Premier League season, Liverpool finished eighth, 32 points adrift of Manchester United and 11 away from European football. Once again, the season had shown how far Liverpool had fallen. The improvement required in 1993/94 from the team under Souness hadn't happened, and Roy Evans had experienced a difficult half-season since taking over at the end of January, winning only five league matches. There was a real danger of Liverpool becoming a mid-table club, so real change was required ahead of the 1994/95 season. Evans had been given several months to evaluate the squad and assess where improvement was required. He concluded that he simply wanted to buy better players and was 'itching to spend'. The manager was also aware that the team's standard of play had declined and that consistency had been a real issue, one that had remained since the beginning of Souness's time in charge in 1991.

However, Evans also made clear that there was a promising nucleus in the squad, and this was undoubtedly true as they headed towards 1994/95. The current season had seen the coming-out party of Robbie Fowler, one of the best young players in the country, who scored 12 league goals alongside Ian Rush – who himself scored 14. Steve McManaman had also had an improved season, once again showing flashes of real brilliance with the ball at his feet. Jamie Redknapp had also developed in central midfield and was becoming a more capable creator. To top it all, David James had finally established himself as Liverpool's No. 1 and had shown that he could be an excellent shot-stopper and future England international. While the club might have declined, there were reasons to be hopeful for Liverpool fans heading into the summer of 1994. It just required the right manager to take the young core at the club, surround it with talent, improve the style of play and get Liverpool back to the top of the table where they belonged, and maybe, just maybe, add a little bit of spice to Merseyside.

Chapter 4

Who Do You Think You Are? – the 94/95 Season

FOLLOWING A difficult first half-season in charge of the Reds, Liverpool manager Roy Evans entered the 1994/95 Premier League season with much to prove. He'd taken over from Graeme Souness in late January of 1993 with the club fifth in the table and guided them to an eighth-place finish. Evans had done much to begin the turnaround, giving opportunities to the young players who had come through at Anfield – which Souness had already begun to do – and re-establishing the 'Liverpool way', but at this point the club had been without a league title for four years, a significant drought for the Anfield trophy cabinet. In those four years, they'd only added the FA Cup in 1991/92. In much the same way Souness had faced significant pressure to reverse the club's fortunes the previous season, Roy Evans would need results in 1994/95 to show the Anfield board room that they'd made the correct choice in returning to the boot-room philosophy.

After what had clearly been a period of evaluation for the new Liverpool boss, change came quickly. Mere weeks after the end of 1993/94, Julian Dicks was sold back to West Ham United for a fee of £300,000. He'd been one of Souness's last major signings and this had signalled a real shift in transfer policy away from technically gifted players towards hard-nosed bruisers. Despite a few good moments in a Liverpool shirt, Dicks never looked like measuring up to the standard that had been historically expected at Anfield and was a logical sale for Evans and his staff. Also leaving Anfield was centre-back Torben Piechnik, another failed Souness signing, who returned to Denmark with AGF on a free transfer in June.

August saw two more depart the club: Don Hutchison – also to West Ham – for £1.5m and Bruce Grobbelaar, who left on a free to join Southampton. Hutchison had rarely featured since his hot spell for Souness during 1992/93, and despite Grobbelaar being a constant feature between the posts since 1981, his performances over the previous few years had become increasingly erratic. It was clear that Evans had decided that David James would be his starting goalkeeper. He'd been signed by Souness in the summer of 1992 as one of the country's most promising young shot-stoppers but had seen his progress stagnate under the former manager as he found starting opportunities increasingly hard to come by, only regaining the starting role once Grobbelaar was injured in February 1992. Grobbelaar remained in the Premier League with Southampton, a team that entertained but were consistently a lower-table club. Later that year, accusations of match-fixing against Grobbelaar would surface, starting a legal battle he would fight until he and his co-defendants were cleared in November 1997. Perhaps the most significant departure from the club, though, was the undoubted legend Ronnie Whelan, who left in September to become player-manager at Southend United in the First Division. Whelan would eventually retire as a player in 1996.

Three players joined the club during the summer as £10m was made available to Evans to improve the quality of the playing staff. First, 19-year-old goalkeeper Michael Stensgaard was brought in from Hvidovre IF in Denmark for a fee of £400,000. At that point, he was the Danish Under-21 keeper, but the youngster would serve as back-up to David James, in the hope that he would develop. However, Stensgaard would never play for Liverpool's first team, following a freak shoulder injury suffered while setting up an ironing board shortly after his arrival. He would be released in 1996 after further recurring injuries, returning to Denmark and battling to revive his career through the application of psychological coaching. Also arriving at Anfield at the beginning of September were centre-backs John Scales and Phil Babb, for £3.5m and £3.6m respectively.

Scales arrived from Wimbledon and would be one of the best examples of Liverpool's 'Spice Boys' reputation that the club would garner throughout the 90s, buying a red Ferrari 355 with the registration plate 'J1 RED'. Subtle. He had a reputation for being a skilful if unaggressive defender. At the time, Evans said of Scales: 'John is big, strong and a great athlete. He's been the steadiest defender in the league for a long time and he'll be a great asset to us.' Phil Babb joined after having featured for the Republic of Ireland in the 1994 World Cup, where Jack Charlton's Republic team reached the Round of 16, losing to the Netherlands. Babb's £3.6m fee made him the most expensive defender in Britain and he would play a significant role in Evans's tactical plans that season, utilising his pace and tackling ability in a new system. When Evans was questioned about the future of Neil Ruddock upon the arrival of Scales, the Liverpool manager made it clear that he wouldn't have had three centre-backs if he didn't want three in the first place.

Liverpool began the season away from Anfield, facing newly promoted Crystal Palace at Selhurst Park. The Reds went one up in the 12th minute thanks to a Jan Mølby penalty after Rob Jones was clumsily brought down after a foray forward from the back. Mølby had faced a challenging 12 months, finding his place in the team repeatedly under threat and struggling with injuries, but this was already a good sign for the season ahead. The second goal came two minutes later when Mølby released Steve McManaman on the break down the left, before the young star angled in on to his right foot and guided a beautiful shot into the far corner from just inside the box. Amazingly, this was McManaman's first league goal for over a year, but 1994/95 would see the complete resurgence of McManaman, as he thrived in a free role created for him by Roy Evans. The scoring calmed down until just before half-time, when Robbie Fowler capitalised on some poor passing in the Palace defence to toe-poke the ball home from outside the box. It was the kind of finish only Fowler seemed to be able to create, the first of 31 he would score for the club that season. Liverpool conceded just after half-time – much to the annoyance of Evans – but normal service resumed in the 60th minute, with Ian Rush scoring his first goal of the season, heading home a Bjørnebye cross after some nice work in midfield by Jamie Redknapp and John Barnes. McManaman scored his second, stabbing home a Redknapp cutback, and Rush completed the rout with his second, nodding in at the far post from a corner as Liverpool began the season with a 6-1 win. All of a sudden, those on Merseyside had plenty to be optimistic about as the season got going.

Eight days later, Liverpool returned home to host Arsenal. Over 30,000 packed inside the famous ground – now featuring the new Kop stand – as Evans named an unchanged line-up of James, Jones, Nicol, Bjørnebye,

Ruddock, Barnes, Mølby, Redknapp, McManaman, Fowler and Rush. The match became famous for featuring the fastest Premier League hat-trick – a record only broken by Sadio Mané for Southampton in 2015 – as Robbie Fowler netted three first-half goals in a little over four and a half minutes. However, to suggest the performance was a one-man show would be misleading, as Rush, Barnes and McManaman looked rejuvenated at the start the season. As Anfield erupted when Fowler scored his third in the 31st minute, you could feel the hope returning to the great club.

Liverpool ended August with a 2-0 win over Southampton at The Dell, with Fowler scoring again, winning a one-on-one with Bruce Grobbelaar after being fed by a Steve McManaman through ball. Barnes scored the second, dribbling at the Southampton defence, and getting a bit lucky with a ricochet, before executing a beautiful turn to guide the ball into the bottom corner with his weaker right foot. Barnes's role had evolved as the season developed, playing in central midfield and being asked by Evans to link defence to attack. Nevertheless, he remained a player of immense quality who was now adapting his game to the demands of the team, having recognised that the club now possessed a considerable amount of young attacking talent. As ever, a consummate professional. It had been a positive month for the Reds and, as August ended, Liverpool sat fourth in the table with three wins from three matches.

September saw the club's form dip somewhat. It was a challenging month, as they faced West Ham United, Newcastle United, and league champions Manchester United at Old Trafford.

The match against West Ham saw John Scales make his debut for the club, partnering Neil Ruddock in defence. Other than that, it was an unchanged line-up for the Reds, but the match saw the Anfield faithful frustrated as Fowler hit the bar, Barnes hit the post and Bjørnebye went close from distance in a 0-0 draw, their first dropped points of the season. Liverpool then travelled to Old Trafford, where they suffered their first defeat. A mistake from John Scales gifted the opener to Andrei Kanchelskis in the 71st minute, an attempted header to David James falling far short and allowing the Ukrainian winger to guide the ball over the onrushing James and into the net, despite Neil Ruddock's best efforts. United scored again two minutes later through Brian McClair, reminding Liverpool how much they still needed to improve to challenge at the very top of the table. However, the 1994/95 Premier League season would at least see Manchester United properly challenged for the title, as their battle with Kenny Dalglish's Blackburn Rovers would go down to the final day, but more on that later.

The Reds closed out September with a 1-1 draw against Kevin Keegan's still highly entertaining – now league leading – Newcastle United at St James' Park, equalising through Ian Rush after Rob Lee had given the hosts the lead just after the break. The match also featured the first league start of new signing Phil Babb, as Liverpool played with a back three of Babb, Scales and Ruddock, creating a 3-5-2 system that would free up Steve McManaman to play as an attacking midfielder, creating the free role he would thrive in behind Fowler and Rush as the season progressed. September also saw Liverpool begin their cup campaigns for 1994/95 with a 2-0 win over Burnley at Anfield in the first leg of the Coca-Cola Cup second round, with Scales scoring his first for the club to open the scoring.

In October, the Reds continued to pick up wins but they remained a good way behind the league leaders at the end of the month, sitting fifth. The month began at Anfield, where the home crowd saw Liverpool come back from 1-0 down to thrash Sheffield Wednesday 4-1, Rush equalising after stabbing home a rebound before McManaman took over, picking the ball up on the left and dribbling past half the Wednesday defence before guiding the ball past Kevin Pressman in goal. McManaman was also integral in making it 3-1, running directly at the defence again, before his shot aggressively deflected off Des Walker and looped in. McManaman scored his second and Liverpool's fourth in the 86th minute, finishing off a Phil Babb cross. McManaman claimed a hat-trick – which he would eventually be denied – but it was a clear example of the growth the young midfielder was beginning to show in the new role he'd been given by Evans.

A week later, Liverpool welcomed Aston Villa to Anfield and came away with a 3-2 victory that saw them lead from the 20th minute on. Liverpool's goals were scored by Neil Ruddock and Robbie Fowler, who bagged a brace with the help of his talented left foot. However, Villa's second goal which turned the match into far more of a contest, saw miscommunication between David James and the Liverpool back line that allowed former Liverpool man Steve Staunton to tap home from inside the box. The defensive errors that had so often cost Liverpool under Souness had hardly been eliminated, despite the departure of Grobbelaar.

Liverpool's next league fixture saw them travel north to Lancashire to face Kenny Dalglish's Blackburn Rovers and, as had often been the case over the previous few years, the Reds ended up second best, coming away from Ewood Park with a 3-2 defeat after Chris Sutton scored two to keep up Blackburn's title challenge. While the result was a disappointment, the game itself was a close affair and showed the improvements Liverpool had made under Roy Evans, who admitted his disappointment that his team hadn't pushed forward more once they had the lead, and had allowed Blackburn back into the match. It was a match fondly remembered for John Barnes's glorious overhead kick which brought the game level for Liverpool at 2-2.

The Reds won their next two league games, scoring three against Wimbledon at Anfield and Ipswich Town at Portman Road, with Evans announcing after the Ipswich win that Robbie Fowler was about to sign a new four-year contract to remain at Anfield. However, the manager was also critical of the performance of the back three, with defence again being a concern. Liverpool were also in action in the Coca-Cola Cup in October, finishing off their second-round fixture against Burnley with a 4-1 victory and winning 2-1 in the third round against Stoke City. They then closed out October with their first appearance of the season on *Monday Night Football*, but were disappointed with a 2-1 defeat in London against Queens Park Rangers, despite a lovely goal by John Barnes, playing a one-two with Rush before placing the ball into the bottom corner with his weaker right foot. QPR's winner was scored by Les Ferdinand – on his way to 24 league goals in the season – who ended up onside and unmarked as Liverpool's defence again looked suspect.

Evans's team bounced back with two wins to open November, against Nottingham Forest and Chelsea at Anfield; however, the Reds wouldn't claim victory again in the Premier League until Boxing Day, as the goals dried up. They drew with Tottenham Hotspur, Coventry, Crystal Palace and Chelsea, scoring no more than a goal in each match, but it was the 2-0 loss on 21 November to Joe Royle's Everton at Goodison Park that was most disappointing, as they conceded to new Everton signing Duncan Ferguson in the 58th minute when he powered home from a corner. Everton scored their second mere minutes from full time, David James coming to punch a cross away and deflecting the ball into the path of Paul Rideout, who slid the ball home to heap further misery on Liverpool. The lone bright spot of this run was victory in the third round of the Coca-Cola Cup, as an Ian Rush hat-trick helped Liverpool to a rare 3-1 win over Dalglish's Blackburn at Ewood Park. Despite the team's declining league form, they remained tough to beat and sat fifth in the Premier League table on Christmas Day 1994, and they were about to go on a great run of form that would see only two league defeats until April 1995.

Boxing Day saw Roy Evans rewarded with a late Christmas present of goals returning as Fowler and Rush combined to give Liverpool a 2-1 win over Leicester City at Filbert Street. The Reds looked set to go 1-0 down when Barnes gave away a clumsy penalty, but an excellent save from David James – now secure between the posts – kept the scores level before Liverpool were awarded a penalty that at the time appeared soft, as John Scales was clattered by Mike Whitlow when they jumped for a header in the box, but that now would almost certainly be considered a penalty. The spot kick was converted into the top corner by Fowler. The young star was then crucial ten minutes later, as he set up Rush for Liverpool's second. Shocking defending saw

Leicester make it a contest again, when a completely unmarked Iwan Roberts headed home from a free kick. The faithful Reds fans had David James to thank for coming away from the East Midlands with a victory, as he made several fine saves in the final five minutes to secure the points.

This victory spurred Liverpool on to make it four league wins on the bounce over the Christmas/New Year period, the first being a 2-0 victory back at Anfield over Manchester City, as they went n m 1-0 up through an own goal by City's Terry Phelan. Robbie Fowler had a rare penalty miss late in the second half but rectified his error with a wonderful goal two minutes later, picking up a ball on the edge of the box from Steve McManaman – who was in superb form throughout this winning run – before turning inside and firing a hard shot into the top corner with his left foot that gave City's goalkeeper, Andy Dibble, little chance. Liverpool moved to third in the table.

Three days later, on New Year's Eve, Liverpool travelled east to play Leeds United at Elland Road and won again, through Redknapp and Fowler, as it became clear that Liverpool would play some part in the title race, either directly or indirectly. What was undoubtedly helpful for Evans was his ability to send out a consistent XI, as his regular selection in the 3-5-2 system was James, Babb, Scales, Ruddock, Jones, Redknapp, Barnes, Bjørnebye, McManaman, Rush and Fowler. As 1994 turned to 1995, the difference between Evans's and Souness's Liverpool was becoming increasingly clear. Under Evans, Liverpool were a fluid, attractive and attacking team, playing a system that was not only tactically challenging for the rest of the Premier League teams but also got the best out of his star players, particularly Steve McManaman and Robbie Fowler, who were flourishing under Evans to say the very least.

January 1995 began with Anfield being treated to a 4-0 victory over Norwich City, as Scales, Rush and Fowler all scored in a fantastic performance that left Liverpool third in the league. Fowler scored two, as he repeatedly garnered comparisons to Jimmy Graves, perhaps the greatest English striker ever to kick a ball. However, Liverpool as a collective didn't play well in their next match, losing 1-0 at Anfield to George Burley's Ipswich Town after conceding in the 30th minute, then struggling to create anything of note during the remainder of the match. John Barnes was out with a thigh strain and his creativity in central midfield was missed, as Michael Thomas played in his absence.

Liverpool's next fixture was the second Merseyside derby of the season, and Evans's team were again frustrated against their neighbours in blue, this time departing Anfield with a goalless draw as most of the 39,000 in attendance left disappointed. Evans complained about the physical attention his players received but the Reds were unhappy about the draw, nonetheless. However, they were successful in their cup competitions in January

1995, opening up their FA Cup campaign with an eventual, if unconvincing, win in the third round, being taken to a replay by Second Division Birmingham City but finally winning on penalties after extra time. The win in the shoot-out more than vindicated Roy Evans's decision to make David James Liverpool's No. 1, with the shot-stopper forcing four misses from the spot. The Reds again needed a replay in the fourth round after drawing 0-0 with Burnley on 28 January, but progressed following the replay at Anfield in February. In the Coca-Cola Cup, the Reds faced Arsenal in the quarter-finals, winning 1-0 at Anfield after a free-kick routine that had clearly been worked on at Melwood. John Barnes squared the ball to Neil Ruddock on the edge of the box, who slid the ball through Arsenal's defence for Ian Rush to finish in the bottom corner past the onrushing David Seaman.

Also of note in January was the departure of Steve Nicol, who left to become player-coach at Notts County as part of Howard Kendall's staff. Nicol had been part of the playing staff at Anfield for 13 years, playing 343 league matches for the club. He'd been a consistent feature in the Liverpool teams of Joe Fagan, Kenny Dalglish and Graeme Souness, but with the arrival of Babb and Scales in the summer and the switch to a back three, had now fallen down the pecking order. One of the more versatile talents of his generation, Nicol would actually continue several more seasons before retiring as a player in 2001.

Back in the league, February saw Liverpool in action three times. Their first league match of the month was away at the City Ground against Nottingham Forest, a club that had rebounded from their relegation in 1992/93 to now sit a few places lower than Liverpool. Unfortunately for the Reds, they drew 1-1 with Frank Clark's team, conceding in the tenth minute after David James came out to challenge for a through ball and was unable to get to Bryan Roy, who stabbed the ball towards goal for a certain Stan Collymore to tap in at the back post. We'll be meeting him again very soon. Liverpool drew level with Forest in added time, Steve McManaman just able to guide Michael Thomas's pass towards Robbie Fowler in the box, who was as composed as ever in guiding the ball into the bottom corner with his right foot. Yet again it was McManaman and Fowler who came up trumps for the club when needed.

A week later, on 11 February, Liverpool drew 1-1 again, this time with QPR, going 1-0 down after Kevin Gallen's shot from the edge of the box squirmed under James's attempt to save it. Rescuing Liverpool this time was John Scales, forward from the back to tap in an Ian Rush cross at the back post. The following week at Hillsborough, against Sheffield Wednesday, Liverpool came back from 1-0 down again, this time scoring two, through Barnes and McManaman, to record their first and only league win of the month. While Liverpool remained tough to beat, the series of three successive draws had seen the club drop out of the title race, down to fourth but 15 points behind Blackburn.

February also saw the Reds continue to make life difficult for themselves in the FA Cup, winning their fourth-round replay with Burnley but then needing another replay in the fifth round after drawing 1-1 at Anfield against Wimbledon. Travelling to Selhurst Park, Liverpool piled on the pressure early and went 1-0 up after John Barnes headed in from around the penalty spot after a Jamie Redknapp free kick. Barnes then set up Liverpool's second goal, crossing in from deep on the left flank for Ian Rush, who stuck out his left foot and just guided the ball past Hans Segers in the Wimbledon goal. The Reds were slightly more comfortable in their Coca-Cola Cup semi-final first leg against Crystal Palace, on this occasion only requiring time added on for Robbie Fowler to find the bottom corner after a McManaman cross from the right found its way to the club's leading scorer.

In March, Liverpool were beaten only once in the league, coming back from 2-0 down at Anfield to eventually lose 3-2 against Coventry City. Evans's team had also been knocked out of the FA Cup a mere three days earlier at Anfield, losing 2-1 to Tottenham Hotspur, thanks to Sheringham and Klinsmann. However, the month saw two fantastic home wins in the Premier League, as the Kop witnessed victory against Kevin Keegan's Newcastle United and, most significantly, title challengers and reigning champions Manchester

United. It was the pairing of Fowler and Rush that gave Liverpool the win against Keegan's entertainers, 2-0. Against Manchester United it was Jamie Redknapp who opened the scoring in front of the Kop, firing a hard shot past Peter Schmeichel with his left foot from just inside the box, following a midfield scramble. Viewers on *Super Sunday* saw the Kop explode with joy. The second goal was awarded as an own goal to Steve Bruce after some nice work from Michael Thomas in midfield led to the ball going to John Scales, who marched forward from the back, before playing the ball back outside to Thomas, who now found himself on the right flank. He immediately cut the ball back towards the box, where McManaman was waiting. His shot cannoned off Bruce and past Schmeichel into the United net. The defeat was a significant blow to United in their battle with Blackburn, one that Liverpool would be involved in again before the end of the season.

Liverpool closed out their league matches for March with a 0-0 draw down in north London against Tottenham – somewhat atoning for their loss in the FA Cup earlier in the month – but it was in the Coca-Cola Cup that Liverpool scored their biggest success of March, as they travelled to face Crystal Palace in the semi-final in London on 8 March, already 1-0 up from the first leg at Anfield. The only goal of the second leg came about through the work of arguably Liverpool's three most significant players in John Barnes, Steve

McManaman and Robbie Fowler, as Barnes's composure in midfield guided the ball to McManaman, who was able to dribble past a challenge and release Fowler from the Palace offside trap. From a tight angle on the left-hand side of the box, there was never any doubt as Fowler fired across the Palace keeper Nigel Martyn and into the bottom corner in an amazing example of the type of finishing that he consistently made look easy. After the goal, Fowler celebrated by turning his shirt round to show his name for all to see. He might have been wearing No. 23, but this was perfect No. 9 play. Palace posed little threat to Roy Evans's team for the remainder of the match and Liverpool had booked a date at Wembley in April, when they would face First Division Bolton Wanderers in the Coca-Cola Cup Final. This would be the club's first final in three seasons, a clear example of the progress they'd made since the appointment of Roy Evans, vindicating the board's decision to move on from Graeme Souness just over a year previously. Liverpool were a club undeniably on the rise again.

In fact, the Coca-Cola Cup Final on 2 April 1995 was Liverpool's first match of the month. Roy Evans led the team out in front of over 75,000 fans at Wembley Stadium. His chosen XI in the 3-5-2 was – as it had been so often that season – James, Babb, Ruddock, Scales, Jones, Redknapp, Barnes, Bjørnebye, McManaman, Rush and Fowler. Liverpool naturally came into the final as overwhelming favourites but the last time they'd played Bolton was on 13 January 1993, when a Souness-led Liverpool had crashed out of the FA Cup in the fourth round. Roy Evans also correctly identified that, aside from John Barnes and Ian Rush, his team was severely lacking in cup final experience. Bolton manager Bruce Rioch set his team out in a classic 4-4-2, with much of the attention being focused on young energetic midfielder Jason McAteer, who was lauded by Ron Atkinson and Terry Venables on ITV as being a more athletic runner than any option Liverpool possessed in central midfield. McAteer was from across the River Mersey in Birkenhead. Also on the pitch for Bolton was future Everton defender Alan Stubbs, who partnered Mark Seagraves in central defence. It was a warm April day at Wembley, with Kevin Keegan on commentary describing the climate as 'more cricket weather than football weather', suggesting it would have an impact on the match.

Liverpool had the majority of the early possession, as you might expect, but seemed unable to create anything beyond some nice passages of play in midfield and a wild shot over the bar by Fowler from the edge of the box, following an error by Seagraves. The Reds maintained control without really threatening at all, quickly cutting off a potential Bolton counter from a corner through winger David Lee in the ninth minute, with Babb and Bjørnebye combining – if unconvincingly – to take the ball away from Lee as he marched towards the Liverpool box. The most noticeable feature of Liverpool's attacking play in the early phases of the match was the continuous movement of McManaman. At times he was in central midfield, before moving into the No. 10 zone, as well as moving into the half-spaces to find room to create. Liverpool began to threaten more, thanks to combinations between McManaman, Redknapp and Barnes, creating a triangle once McManaman moved to the No. 10 zone. One such example led to the ball finding its way to Fowler inside the box, but his left-footed shot to the near post was well saved by Keith Branagan. McManaman was involved again minutes later when he picked the ball up deep in his own half and dribbled down the left flank, before taking on Bolton right-back Scott Green, then cutting the ball back to Ian Rush, who unfortunately blazed the ball well over the bar.

The Reds remained in control and again tested Branagan when Jamie Redknapp played a beautiful long pass 35 yards forward to Fowler, who played it inside to an onrushing Bjørnebye, who fired the ball directly at the Bolton keeper. Only a minute later, however, David James – wearing a cap to shield his eyes from the sun – was forced into his first real action after a cross was nodded down to McAteer, who fired directly into the arms of the opposition goalkeeper. Bolton again tested James in the 28 minute, McAteer lofting a ball over the head of Bjørnebye. As James came out to challenge, he couldn't quite get to the ball in time, so instead made himself an awkward shape, leaving David Lee no option but to attempt the lob, which fortuitously – for those on Merseyside that had travelled south – landed on the roof of the Wembley goal.

By this point in the first half, Bolton had undoubtedly grown into the match and were beginning to threaten, and the 33rd minute saw them almost go 1-0 up after a throw-in from the left found Alan Thompson, whose right-footed shot forced an unbelievable save from David James, guiding the ball on to the crossbar and over as the winger's shot looked to be finding the corner of the net. Kevin Keegan, understated as ever, labelled James's save as one of the best of the season. As Liverpool looked to be losing control, David James threw the ball out to Phil Babb in the left centre-back role. Babb passed the ball inside to Neil Ruddock, who fired the ball forward to Stig Inge Bjørnebye. He managed to control the hard pass and guided it towards John Barnes, who quickly spotted Steve McManaman in space further forward. As McManaman turned and drove into the open space ahead of the Bolton back four, Alan Stubbs and Scott Green came towards him, but at this point McManaman was moving too fast to be stopped and, after he guided the ball through Green's legs, Liverpool's star midfielder fired past Branagan and into the Bolton goal to make it 1-0. As those wearing red exploded around Wembley, it was another undeniable moment that showed that Liverpool were back as a legitimate force in English football once again. McManaman had broken out under Souness, stagnated for a while, but was now reborn in a new role under the guidance of Roy Evans, with more to come.

Liverpool remained largely in control for the final minutes of the first half, with McManaman threatening again with the ball at his feet but firing well over the bar. As a result, they went in at half-time 1-0 up, with the match anything but over. As the teams went in, Roy Evans praised David James for keeping his team in the match and he knew that his team would need to pass the ball better in the second half. In fact, Bolton began the second half positively and almost drew level within minutes, as the ball was played forward down the right flank towards John McGinley. Bizarrely, David James came out of his goal to challenge, despite never looking remotely close enough to the ball and having Ruddock and Babb back to support. Needless to say, McGinley beat James to the ball and squared it for his strike partner Mixu Paatelainan, who had an open goal in front of him but John Scales for company. As Scales battled Paatelainan for the ball, the Finn's shot went just wide of the post, with James scampering back into position. Roy Evans's team had been lucky to say the least.

This showed the issue with David James. So often he was capable of elite shot-stopping, but he was also prone to baffling mistakes, much like his predecessor Bruce Grobbelaar. Minutes later, Alan Thompson threatened the Liverpool goal again, firing just wide with his left foot from just inside the box after McAteer had lofted the ball forward from deep in midfield. Bolton had brought 33,000 fans with them to London, and they began to make more and more noise in the famous old stadium. In the 50th minute, however, Bolton were lucky to still have 11 men on the pitch, after Alan Thompson went flying into McManaman from behind as he received the ball from Redknapp, sending the Liverpool goalscorer flying. Had Thompson made any lasting contact with McManaman, he surely would have been given his marching orders by referee Philip Don. A minute later, Liverpool hit the post after Bjørnebye laid the ball forward to Rush near the byline, with the Welshman playing it back to Bjørnebye as he continued his run into the box. Bjørnebye's sliding shot found its way past Branagan, but it also found the far post. The ball then ricocheted out towards McManaman, who was unable to continue the assault on the Bolton goal.

Bolton continued to have confidence, though, and threatened again in the 56th minute when David Lee was able to cross from the byline and Alan Thompson just needed to make decent contact from within yards of the goal to score, but in the end his header posed no threat at all to David James. The momentum of the match then swung back and forth, with McManaman again threatening, cutting inside from the left wing but firing his shot high and wide as Fowler raised his arms, completely unmarked on the edge of the box. Liverpool now entered one of their better periods of the match, controlling possession in the Bolton half and almost going two up when Bjørnebye – who had a fantastic match – crossed from the left-hand side and Rush showed his predatory instinct to get in between two Bolton defenders to force a great save from Branagan at his near post.

McManaman's dribbling continued to be a consistent threat to Bolton, with the young midfielder driving past the Bolton midfield and finding spaces that were a natural weakness of the 4-4-2. In the 66th minute, this was proven when David James claimed a Bolton cross and side-armed the ball out towards McManaman, who played the ball to Jamie Redknapp. Redknapp evaded the Bolton midfield's press and guided the ball out towards McManaman, who now took up a position on the left wing. He drove forward and went past right-back Scott Green to move into the box, continuing through Seagreaves, who had come out to challenge, and side-footing the ball into the bottom corner. The goal was a microcosm of what made McManaman great in Evans's 3-5-2: his ability to find space, his vision with the ball and his ability to go past defenders with ease. It was 2-0 Liverpool, and the second goal the Reds had so badly needed had finally come.

Bolton immediately pushed forward looking for a response and quicky managed to get a goal back, Guðni Bergsson – who had just come on for Green – heading the ball into the box and finding Paatelainan, who nodded the ball down for Alan Thompson to complete his eventful match by turning and firing the ball into the top corner to make it 2-1. Bolton tried to push forward in search of an equaliser, but while they had a decent amount of the ball, Liverpool managed to regain control and seemed content to look to hit Bolton on the counter. Liverpool's best player in the final quarter was John Barnes, who had adopted a more defensive role and position in the 3-5-2, regularly picking the ball up deep in midfield and, while under pressure from the Bolton midfield, calmly picking the correct passes to allow Liverpool to keep the ball and kill the game. Clearly, that was the cup final experience that Evans had spoken about before the match. On commentary, Keegan referred to him as the 'conductor of the orchestra'. Quite the compliment.

Aside from a McAteer attempt from 25 yards that found its way wide of David James's post, Liverpool managed things in the final ten minutes, never really looking threatened and playing possession football to end the final as a contest. As Philip Don blew the final whistle, Evans, Moran and the backroom staff embraced. Liverpool were 2-1 victors, winners of the Coca-Cola Cup. The trophy was the club's first silverware since Souness's team won the FA Cup back in 1991/92. As the Liverpool fans who had made the journey south continued to chant, 'You'll Never Walk Alone', it was yet another clear example of the progress the club had made throughout the season and since Evans had taken over as manager. They were on the rise and showing plenty of promise for the remainder of the 1990s.

Steve McManaman was unsurprisingly given the man-of-the-match award, having scored two goals and dominated the play with his movement and dribbling. When interviewed, Evans said, 'The two goals were fantastic. Sometimes he does need a kick up the backside, but they were really two great goals.' He further praised his team, stating he'd always felt they had a capable squad, but that this was only the first step and he actually felt his team hadn't played that well – Keegan would disagree on commentary – but he was happy for the fans. Evans was probably right in that it wasn't a classic Liverpool performance and wouldn't have featured anywhere close to their best performances of the season, but it was a trophy win, a win that showed clear progression post-Souness, and continued the positive momentum that Liverpool had built up throughout 1994/95.

The trophy was also Liverpool captain Ian Rush's fifth League Cup, and he also credited McManaman for scoring 'two great individual goals'. When Rush lifted the Coca-Cola Cup trophy – having been awarded the cup by the great Sir Stanley Matthews – there was a huge roar around Wembley. Liverpool were winners once again and, after the struggle of the Souness years, that was the most important thing. It also guaranteed

European football for Liverpool in the 1995/96 UEFA Cup. Finally, Anfield would host European nights again.

Back in the Premier League, Liverpool continued the momentum of the cup final win with four wins from six league matches during April, beating Southampton, Arsenal, Leicester City and Norwich City to finish the month fourth in the table. They continued to entertain fans and neutrals but suffered a major loss in the 3-1 win over Southampton at Anfield when Stig Inge Bjørnebye broke his leg after stretching for a cross from Jamie Redknapp. Bjørnebye had been a consistent member of the first XI and had excelled at left wing-back in Evans's 3-5-2 system, far exceeding his performances over the previous seasons since joining from Rosenborg. He would have to fight to reclaim his place over the coming seasons once he returned from the freak injury.

Also of note in April was the debut of Mark Kennedy against Leeds United. In one of the brighter moments of a 1-0 loss for the Reds at Anfield, he almost smashed the ball into the top corner from 30 yards with his left foot. Kennedy had been signed from Millwall for £1.5m, making him the most expensive teenager in British football history. It would also be one of Kennedy's few bright moments wearing the famous red shirt. He also started in the match against Arsenal at Highbury and featured in the winning goal, laying the ball off for Steve McManaman to work wonders, dribbling past Martin Keown on the edge of the box – leaving the future England international on the deck – before squaring for Robbie Fowler to tap in at the far post in the 90th minute.

May began with Liverpool having virtually nothing to play for in the remaining weeks and set to play Wimbledon, Aston Villa and West Ham United. However, the marquee match-up would be on the final day as Evans's team were scheduled to host Kenny Dalglish's Blackburn Rovers at Anfield. Blackburn, helped by the funding of millionaire Jack Walker, had continued to improve year by year and now found themselves in a battle with Manchester United for the Premier League crown. Liverpool went into the match without a win in the month, having drawn 0-0 with Wimbledon at Selhurst Park, and losing 2-0 and 3-0, respectively, to a struggling Villa and West Ham. Blackburn themselves went into the match with inconsistent form, having lost to Manchester City and West Ham, but beating Newcastle United in their previous fixture, with the only goal coming from the league's leading scorer, Alan Shearer.

On the other side of the equation, Sir Alex Ferguson's Manchester United had remained unbeaten in the league since their 2-0 defeat at Anfield in March. Souness's Liverpool had cost Manchester United the title in 1991/92 and once again Liverpool would have a say in who would win the Premier League. Going into the match, Blackburn were two points clear of United and simply needed to match their result. Manchester United's opponents were West Ham United – recently confirmed safe from relegation – at Upton Park. Speculation was rife that Evans's team would go easy on Blackburn due to Dalglish's status as an Anfield legend, but the Liverpool boss made it clear that this wouldn't be the case.

Blackburn took the lead 20 minutes in, with a Stuart Ripley cross from the right wing meeting the run of Alan Shearer, who fired the ball past David James and into the bottom corner to make it 1-0 Blackburn. News also came in that Michael Hughes had scored at Upton Park to give West Ham the lead. However, Liverpool wouldn't simply submit and allow Blackburn to win the title. They continued to fight, eventually getting the equaliser 20 minutes into the second half when John Barnes deftly side-footed a Mark Kennedy cross from the left into the bottom corner from inside the box. With Ian Rush injured and not named in the squad, Barnes was wearing the captain's armband.

With Liverpool's equaliser, things became tense for Blackburn, as Manchester United now simply needed to win at Upton Park, having equalised through Brian McClair in the 52nd minute. Tension continued to build at Anfield as Manchester United continued to be locked at 1-1 and Liverpool continued to attack. The drama escalated in time added on as Jamie Redknapp curled a free kick from 25 yards past Tim Flowers to put Liverpool 2-1 up. Almost as soon as the teams lined up to kick off, cheers exploded around Anfield as news came through that West Ham had managed to hold Sir Alex Ferguson's team to a 1-1 draw, meaning, regardless of the result, Blackburn were Premier League champions. Dalglish and his staff embraced as the final whistle went and Blackburn celebrated, with Ronnie Moran congratulating the Liverpool legend as he became only the third manager to win league titles with different clubs, joining the elite group of Herbert Chapman and Brian Clough. From Liverpool's point of view, they'd continued to be professional on the final day, and the win against the champions confirmed a fourth-placed finish for the Reds, their best since the 1990/91 season that saw Souness take over in April.

Evans stated that the team had 'let ourselves down slightly' at the end of the season, but it was undoubtedly a season of major progress for the club. The young players that had at times appeared so promising under Souness were now beginning to show that promise on a regular basis. Robbie Fowler was proving to be the best young striker in the country and was rewarded with the PFA Young Player of the Year trophy. He would go on to be a cornerstone of the Liverpool team throughout the decade. Jamie Redknapp had grown in central midfield, improving as a passer and looking set to continue that development. Steve McManaman had also well and truly stepped into the limelight, excelling in the free role given to him by Evans in the 3-5-2, floating all over the pitch and creating at will. Rob Jones had also thrived in the 3-5-2 at right wing-back and was chosen as a defender in the PFA Team of the Year alongside Gary Pallister, Colin Hendry and Graeme Le Saux.

The more experienced players had also fulfilled their roles superbly throughout the season, with Barnes adapting to a new, deeper role in central midfield, and Ian Rush continuing to support Fowler with 19 goals across the season. Evans had also proven to be a capable – if attack-orientated – tactician, making the switch to 3-5-2 that had unleashed Liverpool as an attacking force following the dour years of Souness's reign. The season wasn't perfect, and questions still remained about Liverpool's defence, but this was a huge step forward for the club in becoming a respectable force in English football once again. Liverpool were no longer a fading star and now appeared to be on the rise, back in Europe and on the verge of beginning to compete at the very top of the Premier League table. Captain Ian Rush correctly identified that during the season Liverpool had beaten Manchester United, Blackburn and Newcastle, but had dropped points against lower-half teams. Expectations would certainly be higher in 1995/96, and Liverpool would have to meet those expectations and improve on the fourth-placed finish. Things were about to get spicy on Merseyside.

Chapter 5

Viva Forever – Liverpool in 95/96

AFTER THE significant improvement that was the 1994/95 season, Roy Evans and his Liverpool team entered 1995/96 with a new kind of pressure. After struggling through the Souness era in the early 90s, the club had now finally become a relevant force in English football once again and were now expected to compete at the very top of the Premier League. In short, Liverpool were expected to be Liverpool again. This expectation was mirrored by the majority of the country as the 1995/96 Premier League season began. League champions Blackburn Rovers had failed to significantly add to their squad and had 'promoted' Kenny Dalglish to the director of football role. Furthermore, Manchester United responded to their final-day defeat by selling star players Andrei Kanchelskis, Paul Ince and Mark Hughes and replacing them with a bunch of youth-team players that came through in 1992. It was a crazy strategy. You can't win anything with kids. In the north-east, Newcastle United had gone spending, bringing Les Ferdinand to Tyneside as well as the mercurial French left-winger David Ginola. To all intents and purposes, the Premier League championship looked very much up for grabs.

On Merseyside, there was plenty to be excited about. Firstly, the full squad returned from 1994/95, meaning Evans and his staff simply had to go looking for areas to strengthen, rather than replace. Those weaknesses were certainly more difficult to spot than they'd been in previous seasons. Liverpool's defence had been significantly invested in through John Scales, Phil Babb and Neil Ruddock, and star youngsters Jamie Redknapp, Steve McManaman and Robbie Fowler had properly broken through as a core for Evans to build around as the decade continued. One area that could be correctly identified as a weakness was up front, where Ian Rush – despite complementing Robbie Fowler extremely well in 1994/95 – was ageing and would need replacing in the longer term. The striker the club decided on was Nottingham Forest's Stan Collymore. He'd fired in 22 goals at the City Ground the previous season and his reward was to become a British record transfer as he arrived at Anfield for a fee of £8.5m. Collymore was a fantastic talent and there was little doubt about that fact, but on many occasions he would also be accused of not training well and being too headstrong, especially against more experienced and established colleagues.

Nevertheless, it was hoped by those at Anfield that Collymore and Fowler would be the front two that would fire Liverpool back to their perch on top of English football.

Also joining the club was goalkeeper Stephen Pears, who provided further back-up to the firmly entrenched first-choice keeper David James, and Jason McAteer, signed from Bolton Wanderers for a fee of £4.5m. McAteer had featured for Bolton in their Coca-Cola Cup Final against Liverpool in April and arrived on Merseyside in September, to be converted by Evans and his staff to play as a right wing-back. As a result, the previous season's PFA Team of the Season right-back Rob Jones would be converted to play left wing-back in the absence of Stig Inge Bjørnebye due to a broken leg. With a starting line-up of James, Scales, Ruddock, Babb, McAteer, Jones, Redknapp, Barnes, McManaman, Collymore and Fowler, Liverpool were once again ready to challenge domestically. They would also be sporting a new set of Adidas kits for 1995/96, with the home and away designs easily ranking among the best of the decade.

Liverpool opened the season at Anfield, as Collymore made his league debut for the Reds against Sheffield Wednesday. He partnered captain Ian Rush up front as the newly bleach-blond Robbie Fowler began the season from the bench. Liverpool threatened throughout the first half – with Jamie Redknapp hitting the bar with a thunderous shot from distance – but the Anfield faithful had to wait until the second half for the opener. When it comes it was a glorious one as Collymore picked the ball up 30 yards out with his back to goal and dribbled past two Wednesday defenders before curling the ball into the bottom corner from distance as Anfield erupted. Clive Tyldesley on commentary said, 'You only get what you pay for in this world, and Liverpool have paid top price for a top finisher.' Tyldesley was absolutely right, and if Liverpool could get their strikers firing, it promised to be a great season.

Unfortunately, their next league match was on *Monday Night Football* at Elland Road against Leeds United. It finished 1-0 to the Yorkshire club and was most famous for the unbelievable volley scored by Tony Yeboah, as he blasted the ball in off the crossbar from around 25 yards. Liverpool, however, contended that they should have been awarded a penalty earlier in the match as Leeds defender John Pemberton brought down Stan Collymore in the area. Referee David Elleray, however, waved play on. Even more infuriatingly for Liverpool, the tackle saw Collymore depart with an ankle injury, and the £8.5m signing was unavailable for the rest of the month.

In his stead, Robbie Fowler returned to the starting line-up to partner Rush up front against Tottenham Hotspur. Fowler's return paid immediate dividends for Evans's team, as the previous season's PFA Young Player of the Year scored one of Liverpool's three goals at White

Hart Lane, meeting a Steve McManaman cross in the box and sending the ball into the top corner. Amazingly, the strike was Fowler's 50th career goal. John Barnes scored Liverpool's other two goals, one a beautiful shot into the top corner from 20 yards, the other a wonderfully composed finish into the bottom corner after a pass from Fowler on the counter. The Reds then rounded off August with another win at Anfield, as Neil Ruddock scored a rare goal to give them a 1-0 victory against Queens Park Rangers. With three wins from four matches, the season had started positively enough on Merseyside. There was further good news for the club when it was announced that John Barnes had signed a new two-year deal, keeping him at the club until 1997. Steve Harkness had also penned a new three-year deal, having started the season at left wing-back. In a move that exemplified what Liverpool Football Club stands for, Evans and his staff also showed loyalty to Stig Inge Bjørnebye – whose place Harkness had taken after the Norwegian's leg-break – signing him to a new contract through to 1998.

September opened with a disappointing 1-0 loss to the ever-difficult Wimbledon at Selhurst Park in a match that featured a near brawl between the returning Stan Collymore – partnered with Fowler – and Vinnie Jones, as Jones headbutted Collymore in the ribs, receiving his marching orders as a result. Wimbledon scored a typically scrappy goal for their winner, as Liverpool failed to deal with an Andy Thorn free kick, the delivery going in off Phil Babb to record their second loss of the season. However, they bounced back with a statement victory as they welcomed the Premier League champions Blackburn to Anfield. Liverpool had beaten the Lancashire team on the final day of the 1994/95 season, and they comfortably won this one 3-0.

As so often throughout their history, it was a first-half flurry that gained them the points, with Jamie Redknapp opening the scoring in the 12th minute with a beautiful shot from 20 yards that swerved away from the diving Tim Flowers and into the far corner. Robbie Fowler doubled the lead ten minutes later with a powerful diving header, meeting a wonderful cross by right wing-back Rob Jones. Fowler may have looked different at Anfield with his blond locks, but the finishing was as recognisable as ever – clinical. Liverpool's third was the pick of the bunch, as McManaman turned and squared the ball to Fowler outside the box. Surrounded by Blackburn defenders, he did the same, squaring the ball to Collymore, who immediately struck the ball with his left foot and sent it curling into the corner of Flowers' goal. It was just the type of genius the £8.5m man was capable of, and it signalled Liverpool's progression as a club. Liverpool – not Blackburn Rovers – would be the team to watch for the remainder of the decade.

The match also saw Jason McAteer make his debut off the bench for the Reds, and he impressed in around ten minutes of action. The start of the season also saw the return of Mark Wright to the team, having made only six appearances in 1994/95. Wright had been bought in the summer of 1991 by then manager Graeme Souness for a record fee for a defender of £2.2m but had lost his place due to poor form, attitude and the arrivals of John Scales and Phil Babb. However, 1995/96 would see Wright revitalised, and the ball-playing defender would regain his place in the team, as well as being capped again by England manager Terry Venables ahead of Euro 96. He would only miss out on being part of Venables's final squad due to injury.

Liverpool's next match in the Premier League was against Bolton Wanderers, the team they'd defeated in the previous year's Coca-Cola Cup Final, and Jason McAteer's former club. McAteer started on the bench, however, and it was Robbie Fowler who deserved all the plaudits, scoring four as Liverpool hammered Bolton 5-2 at Anfield. The Bolton defence was poor throughout, but it was Fowler's seemingly innate knack of being in the right place at the right time that contributed most to his goalscoring form. Fowler now had six goals for the season, having been on the bench for the first two matches. As September ended, Liverpool sat third in the Premier League table, three points behind early pace-setters Newcastle United.

Evans's team had also begun their cup campaigns for the season in September. On 12 September, they'd travelled to Russia to face Spartak Vladikavkaz in the

UEFA Cup. After an odd bit of goalkeeping from David James that saw him completely misjudge the flight of a free kick from Mirjalol Qosimov to give Spartak the lead, Liverpool fired back through their young guns. First McManaman equalised after he broke the Russians' offside trap, rounded the goalkeeper, and calmly curled the ball into the far corner from an extremely tight angle. The second was scored by Redknapp, who let fly from 30 yards out, leaving the Spartak goalkeeper Kharpov rooted to the spot as the ball nestled in the corner of his goal. The return fixture at Anfield finished 0-0 as Liverpool made a successful return to European competition. In domestic cup competition, defending their Coca-Cola Cup, the Reds began positively, defeating Sunderland 2-0 in the first leg of their second-round tie at Anfield after two fantastic goals from distance by McManaman and Thomas. David James was also forced to save a penalty – that he himself had conceded – once again displaying his excellent shot-stopping ability. Nevertheless, Liverpool were once again receiving compliments for their style of play and the sheer number of goals being scored at Anfield, consistently rewarding the paying Liverpudlian for their outlay.

October produced yet more goals, as well as an unbeaten month that saw the Reds continuing to remain within striking distance of Newcastle – who were almost unplayable at this point in the season. First up for Evans and his team was a trip to Old Trafford on *Super Sunday* to face Manchester United. After some early scepticism and an opening-day defeat to Aston Villa, Sir Alex Ferguson's youngsters were finding their feet and were unbeaten since that day. The match was also notable for seeing the return of one Eric Cantona to the Premier League following his ban for assaulting a fan at Selhurst Park in 1994/95. However, Liverpool completely spoilt Cantona's return, holding the former champions to a draw. United took the lead through Nicky Butt after a Cantona cross, but Robbie Fowler – partnered up front by Rush – stepped into the limelight and scored two goals either side of half-time to take the lead. Fowler's first was a wonderful strike from just inside the box, beating Peter Schmeichel at his near post. The second saw Fowler out-muscle Gary Neville for a ball into the channel and lob Schmeichel with his weaker right foot. Cantona eventually grabbed the headlines with a penalty after a foul on Ryan Giggs, but it was another match that showed quite how far Liverpool had come under Roy Evans.

Two weeks later, Liverpool were frustrated at home against Coventry, with McManaman the best player on the pitch in a goalless draw. Next up was the difficult journey south to face the struggling Southampton at The Dell, again on *Super Sunday*. The hosts took the lead early in the first half, but Liverpool fired back in the 21st minute as Jamie Redknapp played a searching ball out to the right flank for Fowler, who beat his man and crossed for McManaman to tuck the ball away. The Merseyside club had to wait until the second half to take the lead, but when they did it was again through McManaman, who was first to the rebound after Jason McAteer marched forward from wing-back and had his shot saved by Dave Beasant. Things got worse for Southampton as Le Tissier was sent for an early bath after a second yellow card in the 68th minute, before Jamie Redknapp rounded off a fine away performance in the 73rd minute, breaking into the box and firing past Beasant with his left foot.

Liverpool closed out their league campaign for October against Manchester City at Anfield, having already faced City three days before in the third round of the Coca-Cola Cup. Having beaten Sunderland 1-0 at Roker Park in the second leg of their second-round tie, they proceeded to thrash the struggling City 4-0, with goals from Scales, Fowler, Rush and Harkness. In the league, they were even more dominant, putting six past City, with both Fowler and Rush scoring a brace. Throughout this period, Liverpool's main strike partnership had been Fowler and Rush, with Collymore largely featuring off the bench throughout October. While he'd shown flashes, at this point in the season he'd only scored twice – albeit those weren't just ordinary goals – and Fowler and Rush continued to be a reliable as well as prolific partnership.

Unfortunately, October saw the end of Liverpool's return to Europe, as they fell to a 1-0 aggregate defeat to

SPICE UP YOUR LIFE

Danish side Brøndby IF in the second round. The Reds had been frustrated by a 0-0 draw away in Denmark, then succumbed to a 1-0 defeat at Anfield when Brøndby defender Dan Eggen headed in a late goal from a corner. Evans would state his disappointment at the season's end, explaining that he felt they could have gone much further in the competition than they did.

However, November saw a reverse in Liverpool's fortunes as they went winless in all competitions throughout a month that would be named Black November. It began with a trip to St James' Park to face league leaders Newcastle United, still firing on all cylinders under Kevin Keegan and becoming known across the country as 'The Entertainers'. Newcastle went a goal up within the first five minutes as they piled on the early pressure, Les Ferdinand converting a cross from Keith Gillespie. Liverpool responded within ten minutes as Ian Rush – continuing to partner Fowler up front and keep Collymore on the bench – stabbed the ball in at the far post from a Steve McManaman cross-cum-shot. The Reds continued to threaten and dominate, and were undoubtedly the better team on the day in terms of style of play. Disappointingly for those in red, Newcastle grabbed a late winner after David James failed to properly claim a shot from Rob Lee, Steve Watson pouncing on the rebound to make it 2-1. One claim that's always made about title-winning teams is that they can win when they play badly. Here, Liverpool lost when playing extremely well. At the final whistle, it was noticeable that Keegan said 'sorry' to Evans when the pair shook hands.

The match also highlighted one of the criticisms often laid at the gloves of David James – his propensity for costly errors. Next in the league was the Merseyside Derby at Anfield, where a pair of goals from Andrei Kanchelskis were enough to see Everton win 2-1. The two consecutive losses had a significant impact on the league standings, Liverpool dropping from third to seventh in the table, 12 points behind Newcastle, and now likely out of any potential title race.

Next up in the league were West Ham United at Upton Park, where Liverpool again struggled to convert chances created by their excellent play and came away from East London with a 0-0 draw, despite a match that featured plenty of attacking play. It did, though, see the return of Stan Collymore to the starting line-up as he partnered Fowler, with Rush out injured and unable to return until January. From this point onwards, Liverpool's starting strike partnership would be Fowler and Collymore, with Rush largely used as back-up off the bench.

The Reds closed out a bad month in the league with a trip to Teesside to face Middlesbrough and their Brazilian genius Juninho. The £5m man was part of the move that carved Liverpool's defence open to give Bryan Robson's team the lead within three minutes. Liverpool later equalised through Neil Ruddock, but conceded a second only ten minutes later when Nick Barmby fired past David James. As November ended, Liverpool sat eighth in the table, 14 points off the top. That may not have reflected the quality of their play; but it was the situation Roy Evans found his team in as they headed towards the Christmas period and the turn of 1996.

November also saw Liverpool fail in their defence of the Coca-Cola Cup as they again fell to Newcastle, conceding another late goal to Steve Watson, this time at Anfield. The manager accurately labelled the month as a 'nightmare'. Indeed, it had been the club's worst run of results since 1983. However, they would lose only twice more in the league during the remainder of the season.

There was little sign of this turnaround on 2 December as Liverpool laboured to a 1-1 draw at home to Southampton after going a goal down. Robbie Fowler did almost lob Dave Beasant from 40 yards, but it would be Liverpool's next match against Bolton where they got back in the win column as Stan Collymore scored his first goal since his wonder strike against Blackburn in September, as he took the ball with his back to goal, outmuscled a Bolton defender, dribbled past another defender into the box, before firing the ball past Keith Branagan in the Bolton goal. It was another example of the brilliance Collymore was capable of, only now would he show the consistency that the club needed alongside Robbie Fowler.

On 17 December's *Super Sunday*, Liverpool welcomed Manchester United to Anfield and soundly beat their hated rivals 2-0, with Fowler scoring both, the first a free kick that had Schmeichel rooted to the spot, the second a wonderful finish as he received the ball from McManaman inside the box, feinted to shoot with his left – sending David Beckham flying past the ball – before calmly slotting home with his right foot. Liverpool could – and probably should – have had more too, with Collymore impressive and only being denied by the bar after he forced his way past United captain Steve Bruce. Evans also received praised for sticking with the back three defence despite the absence of John Scales and Neil Ruddock. Rather than moving to a back four, he asked Harkness to move inside to play as centre-back. The manager had faith in the 3-5-2, and there was no need to abandon a system that was both successful and entertaining.

Liverpool's momentum continued in their next fixture as they hosted Bruce Rioch's Arsenal at Anfield. They went 1-0 down after Mark Wright brought down his namesake Ian and the Arsenal striker converted the spot kick. The Reds then fought back, though, with a Robbie Fowler hat-trick to give them a well-deserved 3-1 victory. What's more, all three of Fowler's goals were assisted by his strike partner Collymore, showing the developing partnership between the two. Liverpool then closed out 1995 with a visit to Stamford Bridge to face

Chelsea, coming away from London with a 2-2 draw, both goals scored by the ever-creative Steve McManaman, who continued to flourish in the central role afforded him by Roy Evans. As 1995 turned to 1996, Liverpool had recovered from the shock of Black November to sit third in the Premier League table, but they were still ten points behind Newcastle, who continued to maintain their momentum at the top of the table.

Liverpool's 1996 began fantastically as they went unbeaten throughout January. They started the year by welcoming Nottingham Forest to Anfield and put four past Stan Collymore's former team. It wasn't as easy as it looked for Evans's men, though, as Forest deservedly went two up within 20 minutes, only for Liverpool to fight back through Robbie Fowler, whose brace brought them level before the end of the half. His second was assisted by Collymore, and the pair celebrated together in front of the Kop as they formed one of the country's best strike pairings that season. In the second half, Collymore gave Liverpool the lead when he took advantage of some miscommunication between Forest goalkeeper Mark Crossley and defender Steve Chettle to sneak between the pair and guide the ball home from inside the box. More bad luck followed for Forest as Liverpool made it four after some lovely play in the centre of the park by John Barnes, pirouetting on the ball before finding Collymore, who crossed from the left only to find the boot of Forest's Colin Cooper sending the ball into his own net. Tactically, Collymore's ability to roam the front line in support of Fowler and provide support from the wings – along with McManaman – was becoming a key feature of Liverpool's play, and Fowler was thriving as a result of the support.

Next up for Liverpool was the beginning of their FA Cup challenge for that season, as they duly thrashed Rochdale 7-0 at Anfield. Collymore netted his first hat-trick for the club, another example of his improvement in form. Also on the scoresheet was Ian Rush, making his first appearance since the Merseyside Derby in November. He'd also been awarded an MBE in the Queen's New Year's Honours list, and this goal made him officially the all-time leading scorer in the FA Cup, overtaking Denis Law. The record now stood at 42. Jason McAteer also scored his first goal for the club in the Rochdale drubbing, smashing the ball into the corner of the net after he made a run into the box from wing-back and was found expertly by Michael Thomas. As McAteer wheeled away and was met by Collymore, he held up a finger to the Anfield crowd.

It was Rush on the scoresheet, coming off the bench again, in Liverpool's next match, this time in the Premier League against Sheffield Wednesday at Hillsborough on 13 January. Unfortunately for the Reds, it was only a late equaliser rather than a winner as Wednesday held them to a rare draw during the early months of 1996. A week later, Liverpool resumed normal service as they absolutely thrashed Leeds United 5-0 at Anfield. Leeds had beaten them in the previous meeting between the teams on the second matchday of the season, but Liverpool were simply untouchable in this encounter, going 1-0 up when Neil Ruddock – forward for a corner – met Rob Jones's wonderful cross from the left flank. Robbie Fowler made it two after he converted Liverpool's first – and only – penalty of the season after Rob Jones was brought down when through on goal by Gary Kelly. Kelly received his marching orders from referee Paul Durkin, making Leeds's task even tougher. Fowler bagged his second and Liverpool's third after Collymore – again drifting out to the left-hand side – drove past the Leeds defence and squared the ball just out of reach of goalkeeper Mark Beeney for Fowler to tap in at the far post. Collymore himself made it 4-0 after a hard shot from 25 yards that Beeney should probably have saved, then Ruddock scored an unlikely second to make it five after Leeds failed to clear a corner and it fell to 'Razor' in the six-yard box. Naturally, Ruddock blasted the ball home to loud roars from the Kop.

Over a week later, on 31 January, Liverpool closed out the month with a 2-0 victory at Villa Park against Aston Villa, thanks to two goals in five minutes from star strikers Fowler and Collymore. As January 1996 ended, Liverpool were second in the Premier League table, ahead of Manchester United on goal difference. However, they were still nine points behind leaders

Newcastle United, who also had a game in hand and seemed uncatchable at this stage of the season. What could have been without the collapse in Black November?

January also saw two players leave Anfield. Firstly, Mark Walters left for the still struggling Southampton on a free transfer. Overall, he'd made 124 appearances in the famous red shirt. Secondly, Nigel Clough was also sold to a relegation candidate, this time to Manchester City for £1.5m. He'd been signed by Graeme Souness in his seemingly never-ending battle to replace the productivity of Peter Beardsley, and was a good player who was a victim of circumstance, joining the club at a difficult period in its history, expected to be a player he wasn't. He did have some good moments at the club, particularly his two goals against Manchester United at Anfield in January 1994; however, Clough made just 44 appearances.

February saw Liverpool in action only three times in the league. The first was at Anfield against Tottenham Hotspur, where the home team was frustrated to draw 0-0 in a match where both teams had ample opportunity to win it. This left Liverpool 11 points behind Newcastle. Eight days later, in London, Liverpool left Loftus Road with all three points as Mark Wright opened the scoring with a nice finish after remaining forward from a corner, and Robbie Fowler finished on the break after a wonderful pass from Stan Collymore that split QPR's centre-backs. It was an example of the kind of vertical attacking football that Liverpool were capable of – and often displayed that year. QPR did get one back from Danny Dichio, but Evans's team held on for a 2-1 victory.

Three days later, on 14 February 1996, club legend Bob Paisley passed away at the age of 77. He was survived by his wife Jessie, his sons Robert Jr and Graham, and his daughter Christine. Roy Evans readily conceded that he'd learned a lot from Paisley and that he wouldn't have been where he was without his influence. When Liverpool faced Shrewsbury in the FA Cup fourth round four days later, a minute's silence was held at Gay Meadow and the team wore black armbands in honour of their former manager, who had so expertly developed the club following the stepping down of Bill Shankly in 1974. The performance they gave honoured Paisley in the best way – playing attacking Liverpool football of a kind that Shankly and Paisley had laid the groundwork for. Collymore opened the scoring in the first ten minutes after being played in by McManaman, then Liverpool scored three more after the break, forcing an own goal from David Walton for their second, Robbie Fowler rounding the goalkeeper and tapping in for the third, and McAteer making it four by finishing in the box after another wonderful pass from Steve McManaman.

Next up, the Reds were back in the league, facing Blackburn Rovers at Ewood Park. This clearly wasn't the Blackburn from 1994/95, as they sat sixth in the table, only a point ahead of Forest in ninth. The match is most famous for Liverpool's often replayed first goal, Stan Collymore shooting from about 25 yards and the ball bobbling up off the playing surface and over the waiting hands of Tim Flowers in the Blackburn goal. Collymore made it two with a more deserved goal minutes later, firing into the bottom corner from a free kick just outside the box in what would now be called the left half-space. Blackburn scored through Jason Wilcox to keep the match a contest, but Liverpool made it three through Michael Thomas – having a fantastic run of form post-Christmas – on the break as with his right foot he fired past Flowers, who was unable to stop the hard shot as it squirmed home. Blackburn scored a second through Tim Sherwood to make it close, but the Reds held on to record another victory.

They then finished the month off by progressing through the FA Cup fifth round with a 2-1 victory over Charlton Athletic at Anfield, Fowler and Collymore getting the goals. It had been a fantastic month for both men and they were duly rewarded with joint Player of the Month awards. After a difficult start to the season when Fowler had started on the bench and Collymore had only been brilliant intermittently, they'd now forged a partnership that was arguably the best in the country. Credit also went to Roy Evans, who was awarded Manager of the Month. However, as February ended, Liverpool still remained adrift of Newcastle, nine points behind, and Manchester United had hit form and were now only four points behind Keegan's entertainers, although Newcastle still had a match in hand, even if they were beginning to stutter.

February also saw another player leave Anfield, and it was a much-loved name in Jan Mølby, who left on a free transfer to take over as player-manager at Swansea City in the Second Division. Mølby had struggled with injuries over the previous few seasons – and had suffered badly throughout Souness's time in charge – but remained a player that was well liked at Anfield, making 281 appearances from 1984 to 1995. Paul Stewart also left the club during this period, having joined the club from Tottenham in 1992 for £2.3m, but struggling to make a lasting impact.

As Evans and Liverpool headed into March, they began by welcoming Aston Villa to Anfield. As they had so many times during the season, they simply blew their opposition away, scoring three within the first ten minutes en route to a 3-0 victory, the goals being scored by Robbie Fowler – who bagged two – and Steve McManaman. McManaman's goal in particular came at the end of a wonderful spell of passing. The ball was eventually played into John Barnes in the box, and the old master simply flicked his foot at the ball, sending it floating in the air towards McManaman, who volleyed it home from the right-hand side of the box. Both of Fowler's goals came as a result of his gifted left foot; he fired his first into the far corner from 25 yards and the other from a pretty tight angle past Mark Bosnich in the Villa goal. Liverpool maintained the high level of quality throughout the first half, and this victory kept them within touching distance of the front two, now only six points behind Newcastle, who would lose to Manchester United a day later.

On 10 March, Liverpool were back in cup action in the FA Cup sixth round, travelling to Elland Road to face Howard Wilkinson's Leeds United. In what was an annoyance for the fans in attendance and a compliment in the extreme to Roy Evans and his staff, Leeds played extremely cautiously at home, earning themselves a 0-0 draw and a replay at Anfield later in the month. The Reds did have chances to progress to the semis, but these were often from distance and unlikely to challenge John Lukic in the Leeds goal. In the end, all Leeds had done was prolong the inevitable, as ten days later Liverpool won 3-0 at Anfield to advance, with second-half goals from McManaman (two) and Fowler sealing the win

Unfortunately, while the Reds were successful in the cup, the remainder of their league campaign in March saw them drop points. They only drew 2-2 against Wimbledon at Anfield on 13 March, but importantly, bounced back by winning 2-0 against Chelsea days later through Mark Wright and Robbie Fowler. At this point, Liverpool were five points behind Newcastle – who continued to look shaky – at the top of the table, and five points behind Manchester United – but with a match in hand. The Reds were outsiders for the title, but they were playing some of the best football in the country and certainly weren't out of the race just yet.

On 23 March, however, they travelled to the City Ground to face Nottingham Forest, who at this point were tenth in the table. The match had plenty of tension about it, with former Forest man Stan Collymore given a police escort to the ground, but it turned out to be a disappointing return for the £8.5m man as he was booked and substituted, having struggled to make a lasting impact on the match. Liverpool had almost gone 1-0 up in the first half after Robbie Fowler brilliantly attempted to chip Mark Crossley but was denied by the crossbar, much to his annoyance. Towards the end of the first half, David James's tendency to make crucial errors came back to bite as he spilled a shot from Stuart Pearce right into the path of the onrushing Colin Cooper, who squared the ball for Steve Stone to fire home past a diving Neil Ruddock. The goal was very much against the run of play and, although Liverpool pushed for an equaliser – and were denied a goal that was deemed not to be over the line by referee Paul Danson – they succumbed to a 1-0 defeat, putting an almighty dent in their title hopes. Their next match in the Premier League? Newcastle United at Anfield.

Before that, Liverpool ended March by travelling to Old Trafford to face Aston Villa – for the third time in two months – in the FA Cup semi-final. Robbie Fowler took all the plaudits for his performance, days after being named the PFA Young Player of the Year for the second consecutive year and winning his first England cap ahead of Euro 96. He opened the scoring within the first 20 minutes, guiding a Jamie Redknapp free kick into the bottom corner with a wonderful diving header. Once again, Fowler showed his incredible talent to finish seemingly any chance that came his way. However, the match continued to be even as Villa fought back, but they consistently lacked that cutting edge that Fowler so consistently gave Liverpool – and had done for the previous few seasons.

The Reds had David James to thank on a few occasions, making amends for his mistake against Forest earlier in the month. Liverpool then scored two in the last five minutes, the first from Fowler after a Redknapp free kick was headed out to him and he chested the ball down, let it bounce and then guided it into the far corner with the outside of his left foot. Martin Tyler on commentary simply stated, 'You are looking at a goalscoring genius.' Looking back, it's hard to disagree with his assessment of Fowler's performance, and indeed his season. The second – and Liverpool's third – was scored by Jason McAteer, as he tapped in Steve McManaman's cross on the break as Villa desperately pushed forward. The 3-0 scoreline might have flattered Liverpool but they'd booked another date at Wembley, this time for the FA Cup. Their opponents on 11 May would be Manchester

United. Before that, they faced a hectic Premier League run-in, which would start with the visit of Kevin Keegan and Newcastle United on 3 April.

As 22 players ran out on to the Anfield turf that night in April 1996, they had no idea that the match they were about to take part in would be remembered by many as one of the best games of football in this country at any time in the 1990s. It was also likely a must-win one for Liverpool to have any hope whatsoever of lifting the title come season's end. The line-up chosen by Roy Evans was James, Wright, Scales, Ruddock, McAteer, Redknapp, Barnes, Jones, McManaman, Fowler and Collymore. It was Liverpool's ever-present Robbie Fowler who opened the scoring in the second minute, with Stan Collymore crossing from the byline with his left foot and Fowler meeting the ball with a header unmarked at the back post as Anfield exploded with noise. It was Liverpool's first attack and revealed the kind of defensive vulnerability that had been so often associated with Keegan's team – and would continue to be so in the years that followed.

However, Evans's Liverpool admittedly had defensive frailties of their own, and Keegan's team continued to be lethal in attack, going on to score two in the next 15 minutes to take the lead 2-1. The first was scored by Les Ferdinand, who received the ball inside the box from the dynamic Faustino Asprilla, then turned and shot straight at David James, who was unable to stop the Englishman's powerful shot. The second went to the French left-winger David Ginola, who found himself unmarked on the break and was able to finish with his weaker left foot despite the desperate challenge of Jason McAteer. However, play continued to be end-to-end and Liverpool almost levelled the game at 2-2 when Redknapp fired just wide from 25 yards out. He'd scored from distance several times that season, but this attempt swerved wide just at the last moment.

In the second half, Newcastle had Pavel Srníček to thank for maintaining their lead as he acrobatically saved John Scales's free header in the box, but in the 55th minute the Reds did finally draw level as McAteer played the ball forward in the channel to McManaman, who cut inside before squaring to Fowler as he made his way into the box. He hit a first-time shot with his left foot past Srníček as the Kop erupted with applause. Fowler celebrated by diving headfirst into the goal as he was met by McManaman, Collymore, McAteer and Redknapp. Unfortunately, Liverpool had only been level for a matter of seconds when Asprilla broke the offside trap and cushioned the ball past the onrushing David James – who arguably was too far out of his goal – with the outside of his right foot to make it 3-2.

The Reds continued to fight and attack, though, and brought the scores level in the 68th minute when McAteer picked the ball up on the right wing and hit a beautiful low cross into the 'corridor of uncertainty'. The ball drifted past the entire Newcastle back line and was met by Collymore at the back post. After 70 minutes, one of the most incredible matches in the history of English football was tied at 3-3. What made the match special is that both teams continued to attack – a draw didn't help Liverpool at all, and Newcastle knew they needed victory to match the relentless pace of Manchester United.

Minutes later, David James kept the score at 3-3 when he saved Les Ferdinand's point-blank shot after he'd outfought Steve Harkness – who had come on for Mark Wright at the start of the second half – for a long ball from Philippe Albert. With five minutes to go, Evans went all in, bringing on Ian Rush for Rob Jones, playing three strikers up front. Liverpool continued to push forward, as John Scales played the ball to Rush in midfield, who played it back to John Barnes, who himself squared it to Scales. Scales then played the ball back to Barnes, who now drove forward and played a one-two with Rush that ended up with the pair basically on top of each other just inside Newcastle's box. As the ball came free to Barnes, he noticed Stan Collymore unmarked, coming into the box on the left-hand side, and played it to him. As Collymore took control of the ball with his right he immediately swung with his left foot, firing the ball past Srníček and into the Newcastle goal to give Liverpool the lead at 4-3 in the 90th minute. As Collymore wheeled away in jubilation and Anfield once again exploded with noise, Kevin

Keegan hung his head in disappointment behind the advertising boards.

As the final whistle went and Liverpool came away 4-3 winners, they were still in the title race and had once again shown that on their day they could beat anyone. The team that gained most from the night's football, though, was Manchester United. Nevertheless, the match rightly goes down in history as an iconic one that demonstrated what football can be as a spectacle when the conditions are right. What was of note was Roy Evans's interview after the match, where he said, 'There was a lot of kamikaze defending. You cannot win the championship playing like that.' It might have been an unemotional response after what was an extremely emotional match of football but Evans was right. After the season ended, he commented that the game was 'pure football' though. Andy Gray would perhaps put it best on Sky Sports, saying he was, 'honoured to have been sat here and watched a quite magnificent … game of football'.

Unfortunately, after the elation of victory against Newcastle came the depression of defeat on 6 April at Highfield Road against Coventry City, where Noel Whelan's solitary effort condemned the Reds to a 1-0 loss in a bad-tempered match. Afterwards, Evans accepted that the defeat had probably left his team on the outside looking in, but that they would continue to push. The match also saw Steve Harkness – who had stepped up so often this season, playing centre-back and left wing-back

– suffer a horrific double leg-break after Coventry's John Salako dived in with both feet and caught his standing leg. Unbelievably, Salako only received a booking. In the modern game, the tackle would undoubtedly receive a straight red. By the time that Liverpool won their next league match, on 8 April at Anfield against West Ham United thanks to goals from Stan Collymore and John Barnes, they were eight points behind Manchester United, who had now leapfrogged Newcastle to take the lead in the title race.

In the run-in, Liverpool drew three of their final four Premier League matches, including 1-1 in the second Merseyside derby of the season, which featured another error from David James, as well as a 2-2 draw at Maine Road on the final day that would see Manchester City officially relegated to the First Division. The match was also significant as the one that featured Ian Rush's final goal for the club. For a club that can consider itself to have so many players that are club icons or legends, Ian Rush's name belongs at the very top level along with Dalglish, Paisley and Shankly. He'd received a guard of honour from Middlesbrough earlier in the month for his final match at Anfield, as well as a victory lap after the game, handing his famous 'Rush 9' shirt to the Kop as the famous stand sang, 'You'll Never Walk Alone' to their long-time hero and captain. Rush's goal on the final day against City was his 346th in a Liverpool shirt. He'd played 660 times for the club between 1980 and 1996, briefly interrupted by a spell with Juventus between 1986 and 1988. He'd won the old First Division five times as a player, the FA Cup three times, the League Cup five times and the European Cup twice. He'd also been Liverpool's top scorer eight times. As Rush said his goodbyes to the club, it was a sad moment for all at Anfield. After the season, Roy Evans was asked to sum up Rush as a player. In a word, the Liverpool manager simply said, 'Fantastic.'

As the 1995/96 Premier League season ended, Liverpool finished third on 71 points, seven behind Newcastle United in second and 11 behind champions – yes, again – Manchester United. I guess you can win with kids. However, the gap between both teams somewhat belied the performance of Roy Evans's men that season. Yes, Liverpool had always been playing catch-up during the season, but they'd consistently been in the title race until the final weeks, and if it hadn't been for Black November there's a good chance that they would have been champions. They'd played some of the most entertaining, attacking football in the country and had once again shown that on their day they were capable of beating anyone. The Reds had scored 70 league goals and conceded 34 – a very similar stat-line to Manchester United. Disappointingly, they'd shown a tendency to lose matches and drop points at inconvenient times. Perhaps most importantly for Reds fans, they had reason to be disappointed with third – their highest league finish since the 1990/91 season. Third was definite progress, and with Robbie Fowler finishing second behind Alan Shearer for the Premier League Golden Boot, Steve McManaman topping the charts for assists, and David James being chosen as the goalkeeper in the PFA Team of the Year, there was every reason to think that next year could be Liverpool's year. The club was once again on the up, and three of Liverpool's stars – Robbie Fowler, Steve McManaman, and Jamie Redknapp – would be chosen for Terry Venables's England squad for Euro 96, as English football hit new heights and levels of mainstream popularity in the latter part of the 1990s.

Before Euro 96, however, there was the small matter of the FA Cup Final, where Evans's Liverpool would face the new Premier League champions Manchester United. In an old-fashioned tradition that really has been lost in modern football, both teams released songs ahead of the final. For those who are interested, Liverpool's 'Pass & Move (It's the Liverpool Groove)' would peak at four in the charts, whereas Manchester United's 'Move Move Move (The Red Tribe)' would only reach number six. Liverpool would wear their white and green checked away kit for the final, but it would be their pre-match attire that would grab the headlines – and indeed be what the final is largely remembered for – as the players came out on to the Wembley turf wearing off-white/cream Armani suits and red-striped ties. This decision by the Liverpool players was controversial at the time –

and came to epitomise the 'Spice Boys' label that many of the players were given – but looking back it should be clear that this simply represented an individual choice by the players and also the developing celebrity culture that footballers became part of throughout the 90s, a celebrity culture that would peak with David Beckham becoming a mainstream icon in both the sporting and fashion worlds in the 2000s.

Many of the decisions that would garner the 'Spice Boys' label from the footballing media would seem ordinary in the modern game. Jamie Redknapp married a pop star and – along with David James – modelled for Armani. Jason McAteer appeared in shampoo commercials – something that's commonplace nowadays. Robbie Fowler and Steve McManaman were invited to the Brit Awards in February 1996 by Simon Fuller. Fowler was pictured with Emma Bunton – hence the birth of the 'Spice Boys' moniker itself. However, the choice to wear those suits was simply an expression of decision by the players, something that pretty closely resembled what was happening in British culture throughout the 1990s, as Britpop became mainstream and political and social changes occurred in Britain. There may be stories that paint the Liverpool players of the 90s in a bad light – one of the lighter ones being that in the 1995/96 season, they spent around 20 hours practising goal celebrations – but the choice to wear cream suits really shouldn't be one of them.

The starting line-up selected by Evans was James, Wright, Scales, Babb, McAteer, Redknapp, Barnes, Jones, McManaman, Collymore and Fowler. They would be in their 3-5-2 formation, whereas Sir Alex Ferguson's Manchester United would be in their usual 4-4-1-1, with Eric Cantona in the hole behind Andy Cole. This was a battle between the two teams that had scored the most league goals in 1995/96 – United with 73, Liverpool with 70.

It was clear to all watching where the true creativity would come from for both teams. For United, it would be Cantona as always, and for Liverpool it would be Steve McManaman, floating and drifting behind the front two of Fowler and Collymore, who had struck up a real partnership during the season. Unfortunately for the British viewing public, it wasn't only them that this had been obvious to. Roy Evans and Sir Alex Ferguson were also very aware of this and had set out their teams to focus on limiting the supply to both No. 10s, and restricted their time on the ball with the use of the central-midfielders.

The first few minutes of the final saw the ball going back and forth between both teams, with United having the majority of the meaningful possession and creating the first half-chance when Cantona met a long header from the back by David May with his own head to flick the ball forward for Andy Cole, but the £7m striker snatched at his chance and tried to volley the ball with the outside of his right foot, sending the ball dribbling well wide of David James's goal. Within seconds of this, both teams' gameplans became clear as Manchester United regained possession from the goal kick, only for Cantona to be pressed off the ball by the Liverpool midfield as John Barnes moved the ball to McManaman, only for the United midfield to do exactly the same thing, pressing the creative hub of Evans's team off the ball and sending him to the Wembley turf.

Ferguson's team created the next good chance as David Beckham became more of a presence, forcing the first real save out of David James in the fifth minute. Beckham received the ball from Ryan Giggs on the edge of the box and fired a first-time shot that pushed James into the kind of acrobatic save that saw him named in the PFA Team of the Year, as he tipped the ball wide. By the tenth minute, the match was running very much in United's favour, without the league champions really creating anything, while Liverpool's passing became inaccurate. The advanced positioning of winger Ryan Giggs on United's left flank had also pushed right wing-back Jason McAteer almost level with the back three.

It hadn't been a great start for Roy Evans's men. Indeed, Liverpool's first attempt on goal came from 30 yards out when Stan Collymore fired well over the bar with a shot that wouldn't have looked out of place in a rugby match. After ten minutes, Liverpool did finally get some decent possession and worked the ball forward through the lines with some excellent work by John Barnes and

Jamie Redknapp, leaving Collymore barrelling through against the Manchester United back line, and almost one-on-one against Peter Schmeichel before Phil Neville came in to smash the ball out of play and alleviate the danger for the champions. A minute later, Collymore forced a save from Schmeichel, though, firing from a narrow angle on the right side of the box, with the Danish goalkeeper making sure that the shot went wide.

After 14 minutes came the first bit of work for referee Dermot Gallagher when he was forced to separate Roy Keane and Robbie Fowler, who squared up and put their foreheads together after Gallagher had called for a free kick on Fowler – who had barely touched the ball until that point. Minutes later, it was Mark Wright and Andy Cole that would be speaking to Gallagher after Wright tackled Cole strongly from behind. Then, as Dennis Irwin flew into a tackle on left wing-back Rob Jones in the 19th minute, it was clear that there was plenty of dislike between the teams.

What was also noticeable was the pressing adopted by United, especially against Liverpool's central midfield pairing of Barnes and Redknapp. It often meant that, as Liverpool tried to play out from the back, United's midfield were there to make life difficult for them as they tried to play their normal passing game. If the ball did progress towards McManaman, Roy Keane was there to dispossess him in any way possible. In contrast, Liverpool were sitting off the league champions far too

Roy Evans and Ronnie Moran celebrate the winning of the First Division in 1989/90 with then manager Kenny Dalglish.

Graeme Souness in the Liverpool dugout. Souness would take over from Dalglish, but would see the club go backwards.

The new Liverpool manager Roy Evans shouts instructions at his players in early 1994.

Steve McManaman and Robbie Fowler, the two men who would carry Liverpool under Evans, celebrate a goal in 1995.

Liverpool captain Ian Rush and Robbie Fowler celebrate the winning of the Coca-Cola Cup in 1995.

*With the Coca-Cola Cup won against Bolton Wanderers,
Roy Evans takes a second to celebrate in the Wembley
changing rooms.*

David James posing with a Liverpool scarf ahead of the FA Cup Final. Roy Evans's decision to start James ahead of Grobbelaar was one of his first key decisions.

Roy Evans and the Liverpool staff celebrate Stan Collymore's late winner in the famous 4-3 against Newcastle in April 1996.

Robbie Fowler, Steve McManaman and Jamie Redknapp in the infamous white suits ahead of the 1996 FA Cup Final veersus Manchester United.

Roy Evans and Sir Alex Ferguson lead their respective sides out ahead of the 1996 FA Cup Final at Wembley.

Paul Ince would be Liverpool's big signing ahead of the 1997/98 season as Roy Evans attempted to add steel to the much criticised midfield.

Michael Owen, Liverpool's lightning-quick wonderkid who broke out under Evans following Robbie Fowler's knee injury in 1997/98.

Roy Evans and Gérard Houllier sit together on the Liverpool bench as co-managers ahead of the 1998/99 season.

The press conference in November 1998 that officially ended Roy Evans's tenure as manager of Liverpool Football Club.

much, giving them plenty of time to control the ball in deep positions that certainly weren't harmful but were giving them plenty of confidence. However, as the half progressed, the match largely turned into a stalemate, with neither team particularly creating much as they both cancelled each other out tactically. The end of the first half saw Manchester United again wrestle control of the match away from Liverpool, but still they couldn't create anything of note to threaten David James. It was actually Liverpool who created the only other chance of note before half-time when Jamie Redknapp blazed well over the bar from within the United box. However, as the teams went in after 45 minutes of largely dull tactical football, the scoreline read 0-0.

The second half started with Manchester United having their best chance since the opening minutes, as Cantona forced a fantastic save from James when the Frenchman won the ball after a deep cross from Beckham and fired low on the volley towards the near post. James saved Cantona's initial attempt and had Jason McAteer to thank as the wing-back got in ahead of Cole to clear the rebound. The front three of Fowler, Collymore and McManaman continued to work hard, but the gap between them and the midfield was growing with every minute as they became increasingly isolated from the rest of the team. Nevertheless, the ball continued to swing from side to side as neither team could maintain any real control. For both, the majority of the attacking input came from corners that were – on the whole – dealt with effectively by the defence.

Redknapp had another effort from distance in the 56th minute, but in an effort that summed up the match, he simply didn't execute it with the quality required. Then any potential quality was routinely squashed out by both teams when Dennis Irwin took down Robbie Fowler in the 57th minute, and Phil Babb destroyed any potential for a Manchester United counter-attack in the 60th minute by clattering David Beckham to the floor after he'd been released by Giggs. Babb received a booking for his trouble. Roy Keane also grew in importance throughout the second half, continuing to mark McManaman extremely effectively, limiting his creative output. McManaman had been vital for Liverpool throughout the season, and this match was showing just how much the team relied on him.

In the 74th minute, Evans made his first change, bringing on Ian Rush for what would be his last appearance for the club, and taking off Collymore. Rush received an appropriately loud ovation from the Reds who had travelled south, as he slotted in alongside Fowler as Liverpool remained in the 3-5-2 system. Both teams continued to push but created little, with one of Liverpool's better attempts in the second half being McManaman scuffing a shot well wide of Schmeichel's goal from the edge of the box. In the 85th minute, Manchester United won a corner after a pass by Nicky

Butt was intercepted in the box by Babb and cleared. The corner was taken by David Beckham and was aimed at the penalty spot, curving away from goal. David James came out to claim the ball but was forced to flap at it, resulting in the ball ricocheting off Rush into the path of Eric Cantona, who backpedalled and turned his body to fire the ball back towards goal, somehow missing every Liverpool shirt in the box to give United the lead with five minutes remaining.

Evans responded by bringing on Michael Thomas for Rob Jones as Liverpool looked for an equaliser, but they weren't able to create anything before the final whistle blew. In the end, it was a disappointing 1-0 loss after a poor match for all involved. As Liverpool walked up the famous Wembley steps to claim their runners-up medals, they were starting to feel a little bit like the bridesmaid. Manchester United were becoming the team of the 90s, and Liverpool would need to make that step up to challenge them for domestic honours.

As the 1995/96 season ended for Roy Evans's Liverpool, it had undoubtedly been a successful one, but one that perhaps had promised more. They'd been in the title race throughout the season and had once again shown they had the ability to beat anyone. They'd also demonstrated their ability in the domestic cups after their Coca-Cola Cup triumph in 1994/95, challenging Manchester United for a full 90 minutes at Wembley in the FA Cup Final in 1995/96. There was now no comparison whatsoever between Roy Evans's Liverpool and Graeme Souness's Liverpool. The team now played entertaining, attacking football that was loved by the fans as well as the general public and they had shown that they were capable of winning the league. They also had a nucleus of talented players such as McManaman and Fowler who were still young and would improve further.

As stated above, though, Liverpool were increasingly looking like the bridesmaid that was never the bride, while Sir Alex Ferguson's Manchester United had now won three of the four Premier League titles since the break from the Football League and were well and truly entrenched as the country's dominant team. Liverpool would need to avoid their irritating habit of dropping points at crucial times in 1996/97, because expectations would undoubtedly rise again, and Manchester United's young team would only get better as the 1990s progressed. Maybe Liverpool just needed to add a little more spice.

Chapter 6

Spice World – Challenging in 96/97

AFTER THE continued growth and promise – yet disappointment – that was Liverpool's 1995/96 season and a third-place finish in the Premier League, Roy Evans and his staff began the 1996/97 season with even higher expectations. Having recovered post-Souness to be a team fighting in the upper portion of the table, the Reds were now expected to challenge at the very top. Euro 96 had taken place in England that summer – with three Liverpool players featuring in the squad in Robbie Fowler, Jamie Redknapp and Steve McManaman, McManaman in particular featuring consistently throughout the tournament – and English football was becoming mainstream news as the 90s entered its heyday with Britpop, the Spice Girls and Cool Britannia. Liverpool were developing the infamous 'Spice Boys' reputation – fairly or unfairly – and would certainly have to make improvements in the coming season to dethrone the Premier League champions Manchester United, who had effortlessly and seamlessly moved on from one generation to another in the span of one season, creating a new core of talent around the famous Class of 92. This Liverpool team certainly had the talent to be champions and had proved it on several occasions, but they just needed to finally do it when it really mattered.

Meanwhile, Newcastle United had responded to their gradual collapse the previous season by breaking the world record to sign England captain Alan Shearer from Blackburn Rovers for £15m. They'd beaten Manchester United to his signing and could now feature any two of Shearer, Ferdinand, Asprilla and Beardsley up front. They certainly didn't appear to be done as title challengers. Last year's mid-table finishers Middlesbrough had also splashed out, bringing in names such as Emerson and Fabrizio Ravanelli for £4m and £7m respectively. Former Liverpool manager Graeme Souness was also back in the Premier League, appointed at Southampton. Chelsea had responded to the appointment of Glenn Hoddle as England manager by promoting Ruud Gullit to be player-manager, while Arsenal sacked Bruce Rioch just prior to the start of the season. In one of the great what ifs of English football, they would be linked to the former Barcelona manager Johan Cruyff, but would eventually appoint a relatively unknown Frenchman in October. Arsène who?

Liverpool had a fairly quiet summer in the transfer market, bringing in two players, only one of whom would feature in the first team in 1996/97. Australian Nick Rizzo was the player not to feature for Liverpool that year, being brought in from semi-professional club Sydney Olympic on a free. He would never play a league game for Liverpool before joining Crystal Palace in 1998. On a brighter note was the signing of Patrik Berger from Borussia Dortmund for £3.25m. He'd impressed for the Czech Republic in Euro 96 as the young country made its way to the final, where they lost to Germany in extra time. Incidentally, Liverpool had also been interested in his team-mate Karel Poborský, but he'd elected to join Manchester United. Berger had featured mainly as a substitute for Dortmund under Ottmar Hitzfeld but had impressed in an attacking midfield role during the summer's tournament. Long-term, the issue for Berger would be that Evans clearly saw him as a pure striker, but more on that subject later.

Completing the club's quiet summer, the only player leaving Anfield was Stephen Pears, who joined Hartlepool United on a free transfer after providing back-up for Liverpool's starting goalkeeper David James in 1995/96. Perhaps one of the most important names to return to the Liverpool line-up was left wing-back Stig Inge Bjørnebye, who would once again be available full time following the freak leg-break he suffered back in April 1995 against Southampton. Rob Jones had been converted to play the role in Bjørnebye's absence but the Norwegian would regain his place in 1996/97, playing 52 times across the season.

Bjørnebye actually began the season in Evans's starting XI when Liverpool travelled north to Teesside to face Bryan Robson's Middlesbrough, who had finished 1995/96 in 12th place in the table. The line-up was James, Wright, Babb, Matteo, McAteer, Thomas, Barnes, Bjørnebye, Collymore, Fowler. Also of note was the naming of one Jamie Carragher on the team sheet, as he started on the bench in his first selection for the first team. Bjørnebye marked his return with an immediate impact, scoring the opener – and his first for the club – in the fourth minute after running on to a Collymore flick-on and firing past Alan Miller with his left foot. Liverpool were then pegged back midway through the first half, as Fabrizio Ravanelli scored his first of the afternoon from the spot. The Reds regained the lead just minutes later, though, when John Barnes deftly controlled a Jason McAteer cross inside the box, before stabbing the ball into the Middlesbrough net to make it 2-1. Ravanelli brought the Teessiders level before the break, as Middlesbrough took a quick free kick, exploiting a disorganised Liverpool defence, with the Italian sliding in to finish off Neil Cox's low cross.

In the second half, Liverpool took the lead again, with Bjørnebye again featuring, crossing in from the left flank for Fowler to guide it expertly in at the back post with his weaker right foot. Collymore had a chance to secure the result in the latter stages, but frustratingly for the Reds, that man Ravanelli again brought Middlesbrough level as he and Juninho pushed forward in tandem. The former Juventus man then almost won the match for Middlesbrough, but David James saved well at close range, meaning Liverpool escaped the North-east with a 3-3 draw. Once again, they'd shown plenty of capability in front of goal, but fallen victim to defensive lapses. Evans stated after the match that his defence should have cleared the ball several times before Ravanelli scored the final equaliser.

Just two days later, Liverpool welcomed Arsenal to Anfield. Arsenal were a club in turmoil and travelled to Merseyside with Stewart Houston as caretaker manager. The Reds had to wait until the second half to open their home account for the season, scoring through Steve McManaman – now wearing the famous No. 7 shirt – whose deflected shot completely evaded a diving David Seaman. McManaman then made it two within ten minutes, as he dribbled aggressively at the Arsenal back line, before backheeling it to John Barnes, whose shot come back off Seaman directly into McManaman's path, leaving the goal wide open for him to finish. In contrast to the club they would soon go on to become, Arsenal arrived at Anfield seemingly intent on limiting Barnes and McManaman, and therefore Liverpool. Soon there would be a French revolution of sorts that would change English football permanently. For Liverpool, the win certainly hadn't been that convincing and five days later they laboured to a 0-0 draw against newly promoted Sunderland at Anfield, in a poor performance that saw Stan Collymore criticised and David James praised for keeping the scores level, saving twice from Niall Quinn. As August ended, Liverpool were sixth in the table, unbeaten thus far, but with only one win from their first three league matches.

Fortunately for those in red on Merseyside, September saw Liverpool bounce back in abundance, winning every single match they played during the month. In the Cup Winners' Cup, they began their campaign by beating Finnish side MyPa 47 – full name Myllykosken Pallo -47 – 4-1 on aggregate, with a 1-0 win away in Finland being followed up by a 3-1 victory back home at Anfield. The 1-0 victory in Finland was an extremely hard-fought one and was an example of the struggles faced by many of England's finest in European competition throughout the mid-1990s as English football dealt with a post-Heysel ban hangover, being at times tactically and technically inferior to other European leagues. The 3-1 home win was notable, however, for the performance of new signing Patrik Berger, who scored in the comfortable victory. However, Evans lost the services of Mark Wright during the match, the centre-back suffering a fractured cheekbone, meaning he would be out for around six weeks.

Back in the Premier League, Liverpool opened the month on 4 September against early strugglers Coventry City at Highfield Road. However, Ron Atkinson's team were no pushovers, and it took until the 23rd minute of the second half for Liverpool to get the breakthrough, which came through an unlikely source in Phil Babb, who scored his first goal since joining the club in 1994, guiding home a cross from Jason McAteer following a free kick. Three days later, Liverpool returned home to Anfield and welcomed Southampton, now managed by Graeme Souness. He arrived back to a smattering of boos as he took his place in the away dugout. Clearly, many on Merseyside were still to forgive him for his actions during his spell in charge of the great club. Souness's team gave Liverpool a battle, though, levelling the score in the 58th minute through Jim Magilton after Stan Collymore had given Liverpool the lead towards the end of the first half, tripping as he received the ball from John Barnes – regularly finding himself higher up the pitch in the early stages of the season – but somehow guiding the ball into the back of the net. It then took until the 89th minute for Liverpool to finally grab the winner in front of the Kop, as Steve McManaman intercepted an atrociously placed back-pass from Neil Heaney and rounded the onrushing Dave Beasant to finish the match off. The victory put Liverpool up to third in the table and also saw Patrik Berger's league debut for the club.

Next up in the league were Leicester City at Filbert Street, a match that would see the real arrival of Patrik Berger in English football, as he came on for Stan Collymore at half-time with the game in deadlock. He opened the scoring in the 58th minute after Steve McManaman dispossessed Julian Watts as he tried to bring the ball out from defence for Leicester. Berger immediately fed McManaman as the ball rolled free, overlapped the new No. 7 and smashed the ball home following a perfectly timed pass. The Reds doubled their lead mere minutes later, when Stig Inge Bjørnebye crossed from the left-hand side of the box and Michael Thomas's first-time volley squirmed underneath Kasey Keller in goal. Berger finished off the dominant win with his second, picking the ball up 25 yards from goal and simply driving past the defence before again blasting the ball into the back of the net. Keller openly admitted that he'd never seen a ball move as quickly as Berger's two goals on that day. He may have been more of an attacking midfielder than a striker, but Evans spoke about the difficulty a defence faced having to pick up a player like Berger, playing in a deeper role. From a logical point of view, the idea of playing a deeper-lying striker alongside Robbie Fowler made complete sense; the question was whether this would fit with the free role given to Steve McManaman and whether Berger could make it work on a consistent basis. Nevertheless, his performance was impressive, with John Barnes praising him for his vision, awareness and ability to play one-twos. Barnes also made the dramatic statement that Berger could go on to become one of the Anfield greats.

He was on the scoresheet again in Liverpool's next match as they hosted Chelsea. The Czech striker was in the starting line-up, with record signing Stan Collymore finding himself on the bench. It was Liverpool's new No. 9 Robbie Fowler – having taken Rush's legendary number – who opened the scoring, guiding home a wonderful cross from Bjørnebye, who had once again made the left-wing-back spot his own in the 3-5-2. The Reds had to wait until just before half-time for their second goal, as Dominic Matteo pressed a slow pass from Chelsea in the centre of the park, before driving forward with the ball and laying it off to Berger, who rounded Kevin Hitchcock in the Chelsea goal to make it two. Chelsea were further embarrassed before half-time when Andy Meyers headed into his own goal while attempting to cushion a Bjørnebye cross back to Hitchcock.

The second half didn't see Chelsea's fortunes improve, as they were once again caught in possession in their final third, this time by McManaman. Berger picked up the loose ball before guiding it into the corner of Chelsea's goal for his second – and fourth in two matches. His goalscoring efforts would see him named Premier League Player of the Month for September. Captain John Barnes scored Liverpool's fifth in the 57th minute, his volley being deflected past Hitchcock, and although Chelsea avoided a shutout by scoring through a Frank Leboeuf penalty in the final five minutes, it was an utterly dominant performance by the Reds, full of attacking intent. Indeed, it was perhaps one of the best performances of Evans's tenure as manager at Anfield. He made a very clear statement after the match by saying they could certainly have played better.

When Liverpool closed out the month with a 2-1 away win at Upton Park against West Ham United, they were top of the table, with Manchester United at Old Trafford up next. Unfortunately for Evans, Robbie Fowler had missed the trip to West Ham with injured ribs and Stan Collymore went off with a knee injury after giving Liverpool the lead. Ahead of their biggest match of the season, Liverpool would at the very least be without Fowler up front, and Collymore was questionable.

Fortunately, Collymore was available for the titanic clash at Old Trafford, meaning that Liverpool were unchanged from their trip to London. Manchester United featured Karel Poborský in their starting line-up, as well as Jordi Cruyff, who had joined that summer from Barcelona, following his and his father's departure from the Catalan giants. As the match began, four points separated the clubs, meaning this was a match Sir Alex Ferguson's team really couldn't afford to lose at this early stage of the season. The first half saw more examples of David James's interesting decision-making as he came at least 20 yards out of his box to challenge United's Ole

Gunnar Solskjær, who appeared to be through on goal. James managed to use his upper body to block Solskjær's attempt to poke the ball past him, and was then saved by his defence when Poborský immediately fired towards goal from the rebound. The ball spooned up into the air, with James jumping for it but only managing to palm it into the path of a recovered Solskjær, who fortunately was unable to beat Michael Thomas as he came out to press the Norwegian.

The uncertainty caused by James is something that has been mentioned more than a few times throughout previous chapters and would remain an issue despite his excellent shot-stopping abilities. However, as Manchester United pushed forward, they eventually took the lead partway through the first half when the ball fell to David Beckham after Solskjær continued to cause problems for the back three. The young midfielder perfectly struck the ball into the bottom corner, displaying the technique that would be his trademark for the remainder of his career. Liverpool's main threat in the first half was almost entirely Steve McManaman, with his movement causing the United defence some issues – especially with Roy Keane out of the team – the most notable being a classic mazy run and shot that Peter Schmeichel unfortunately saved easily.

The second half saw Liverpool threaten more, with Barnes going close with a header following a free kick, and McManaman blazing just wide after Eric

Cantona was caught in possession well inside United's half. Liverpool almost drew level from the head of Gary Neville when he forced a wonderful save out of Schmeichel after beating Patrik Berger to the ball but nearly guiding it delightfully into the far corner. Later, Schmeichel was once again forced to save, this time at point-blank range from Collymore after he'd collected a cross from Jason McAteer, as Liverpool really pushed down the wings. Minutes later, Schmeichel again saved from the white-hot Berger, who really should have done better, opting to use the outside of his left foot but rather weakly firing right at the Dane. For all of Liverpool's pressure, they couldn't finish the chances they created, so suffered their first defeat of the season, dropping to third in the table. After the match, Sir Alex Ferguson claimed that Liverpool hadn't created much and his centre-backs hadn't had much to do. This was undoubtedly untrue and was likely mind games from the Scot, which the Premier League had already seen him use against Kevin Keegan and would peak during his battles with Arsène Wenger. However, Liverpool had lacked something at Old Trafford – Robbie Fowler. It's hard to imagine Fowler missing many of the chances that Collymore and Berger failed to convert in the second half.

The Reds only played one more league match in October, spending the majority of the month in action in cup competitions. They again progressed in the Cup Winners' Cup, defeating Swiss team FC Sion 8-4 on aggregate over two legs, with the Anfield crowd being treated to nine goals in the second leg in a 6-3 victory. Anfield would have to wait until March for the next round, but the legendary ground would be hosting the latter stages of European football once again. In the Coca-Cola Cup, Liverpool laboured to a 1-1 draw with Charlton Athletic at The Valley and were then forced into an unneeded replay in November that they would win 4-1 at Anfield. The first leg against FC Sion saw the return of Robbie Fowler to the line-up, and he was back in league action against Derby County on 27 October. In fact, Liverpool had their No. 9 to thank for a 2-1 victory, as he capitalised on a rebound from a Patrik Berger shot to finish calmly past Derby's Russell Hoult early in the second half. Minutes later, Fowler scored a second, as he expertly guided a John Scales cross into the far corner with his head. Derby scored a late consolation, but Fowler's return showed exactly what they'd been missing against United, and just how much he meant to Liverpool. By this point, it was clear that Collymore had lost favour with Evans due to inconsistent form, the preferred front two at this point in the season being Fowler and Berger. Nevertheless, as October became November, Liverpool were third in the table, only one point behind the top two of Arsenal and Newcastle, and they had a match in hand on both.

As November began, however, Liverpool stumbled to a 3-0 defeat at bottom-placed Blackburn Rovers, themselves struggling to adapt to life after Alan Shearer. At times the Reds were simply outfought and Blackburn put on their best performance of the season, forcing Evans to adapt his team throughout, moving Michael Thomas to right wing-back to combat the threat of Jason Wilcox and Graeme Le Saux. Blackburn scored two first-half goals through Chris Sutton and Wilcox, and although Liverpool came into the match more in the second half, Blackburn scored a third through Sutton to send Liverpool to their worst defeat in a year and a half. Phil Babb had a torrid afternoon, being the one to concede the penalty in the first few minutes and giving the ball away just outside Liverpool's penalty area, leading to the second goal. Liverpool still had a match in hand over leaders Newcastle United but were now four points adrift.

After winning their Coca-Cola Cup replay against Charlton, Liverpool travelled to Yorkshire to face a struggling Leeds United – featuring one Ian Rush in their line-up – at Elland Road. Leeds had started the season slowly and sat in 17th place, and the Reds did them no favours, rebounding to win 2-0 through goals from Neil Ruddock – returning in place of Phil Babb – and Steve McManaman, who scored in the final minutes when Leeds goalkeeper Nigel Martyn failed to control a long clearance and might as well have passed the ball to McManaman, who ran past him to shoot into the empty net.

Next up, the Merseyside derby, which Liverpool hadn't won since March 1994, not long into Evans's tenure as manager. Unfortunately for those in red on Merseyside, Anfield would still have to wait for a derby win, with an improving Everton holding Evans's team to a 1-1 draw, scoring a late equaliser after Robbie Fowler had given Liverpool the lead with another wonderfully placed header after half an hour. Duncan Ferguson's return to action caused mayhem among the Liverpool defence, and their usual composure and tempo on the ball dipped below standard during the second half. Also disappointing for Liverpool was the departure of Steve McManaman after 17 minutes, limping off with a hamstring injury. He was unavailable for the next league match against Wimbledon, which saw a shocking performance by the Reds, who stuttered to a 1-1 draw, with Anfield booing the team following Øyvind Leonhardsen's equaliser in the second half. The draw was even more disappointing as they would have gone top of the league had they won, with Newcastle only managing to draw against Chelsea. Despite Stan Collymore's record goal after only 33 seconds of the match, Liverpool remained third, one point off the top.

Liverpool closed out November with what was perhaps a welcome break from the Premier League, as they hosted Arsenal – without Dennis Bergkamp – and their new manager Arsène Wenger in the fourth round of the Coca-Cola Cup. Wenger had his new team sitting second in the league and they started well at Anfield, taking the lead early through an Ian Wright penalty after a calamity of errors that saw Neil Ruddock miscontrol the ball and give it to Arsenal's John Hartson, who was then subsequently brought down in the box by the diving David James. Liverpool almost equalised through Patrik Berger, whose shot from the edge of the box somehow hit the post, before rolling tantalisingly across the goal line and out for a goal kick. However, they did finally level things after a wonderful effort from Robbie Fowler, who willingly dived in to stab the ball away from two Arsenal players and get the ball to Stig Inge Bjørnebye, who crossed perfectly for the returning Steve McManaman to loop the ball into the far corner off his head. Fowler then gave Liverpool the lead in the 39th minute from the penalty spot after Lee Dixon was somewhat harshly judged to have handled the ball. Nevertheless, Liverpool should have had a penalty less than a minute earlier after Fowler was clattered by John Lukic as they both chased after a McManaman through ball.

The second half saw Liverpool extend their lead after some fantastic work on the right flank by McAteer and McManaman, with McAteer cutting the ball across the box for Fowler to slide in at the back post. It's difficult to express just how much better Liverpool were during this period when both McManaman and Fowler were on the pitch together. Arsenal did grab a goal back, again from the penalty spot and again through Ian Wright, as Mark Wright was judged to have fouled Hartson when jumping for a cross. However, Liverpool restored their two-goal cushion four minutes later when Patrik Berger scored a trademark drive from outside the box, leaving Lukic rooted to the spot as the ball found the bottom corner in front of the Kop. As the final whistle went, a roar went up around Anfield, in complete contrast to the reaction to the draw against Wimbledon. It was once again a display of what Evans's team were capable of when everything was going right.

The Reds opened December with a journey south to London to face Tottenham Hotspur at White Hart Lane. Roy Evans named an unchanged team from the 4-2 victory against Arsenal, with Fowler and Berger again leading the line. Two goals either side of half-time kept them second in the table, the first a lovely finish by Michael Thomas from just inside the right-hand side of the box, following a glorious defence-splitting pass from club captain John Barnes. Liverpool's second, after half-time, was somewhat fortunate, as Steve McManaman's shot from 20 yards skipped up off the White Hart Lane turf and over the body of the diving keeper Ian Walker. McManaman was easily the best player on the park throughout the 90 minutes, and even claimed that he'd been practising shots in training that would take a late bounce over goalkeepers. I wouldn't take his word for it. With Newcastle losing at home to Arsenal, Liverpool were now three points off the top, but once again with a crucial match in hand.

They next welcomed Sheffield Wednesday – featuring Liverpool favourite Steve Nicol – to Anfield on 7 December. Liverpool were again unchanged, but it was Wednesday boss David Pleat who seemed to get the better of the tactical battle, simply focusing on cancelling out Steve McManaman – pretty much what every team that had been successful against Liverpool over the past few years had done – and sitting deep. From a modern viewpoint, it's clear that Liverpool needed an additional creative source as well as McManaman, but at the same time the team was filled with capable passers, such as Barnes, Thomas and Bjørnebye. Despite this, they were unable to break down a Wednesday defence that worked extremely hard after taking the lead with Guy Whittingham's sliding finish in the 21st minute. Evans admitted after the match that they needed more options when McManaman was being man-marked, and they certainly shouldn't be relying on the attacking midfielder to be the sole creative hub for the team. This is perhaps where a fellow No. 10 to accompany McManaman behind Fowler in some kind of 3-4-2-1 would have been useful, but this was a Premier League in 1996/97 where playing a back three was still out of the ordinary for English football, never mind playing two No. 10s and a back three.

Just days later, one of the former regular members of that back three left the club, when John Scales joined Tottenham for £2.6m. He'd only made seven appearances in 1996/97, drastically declining from 49 and 38 in 1994/95 and 1995/96 respectively, and he'd lost his place in the rotation to Dominic Matteo, with Wright, Babb and Ruddock the preferred option to start. In the Premier League table on 9 December, Liverpool were now four points behind leaders Arsenal, a club completely revived and undergoing a French revolution.

Liverpool's next two matches finally saw them start to produce again at Anfield in the league as they firstly beat a now struggling Middlesbrough 5-1, with Stan Collymore returning to the line-up as Patrik Berger was out with illness. It was Collymore's direct running that set up Robbie Fowler for one of his four goals for the afternoon, as he ran through almost the entire Middlesbrough midfield before laying the ball through their defence for the onrushing Fowler to coolly finish within the first minute. Fowler's second was his 100th goal for the club, scored in only 165 appearances, beating the record of Ian Rush. It was a match that showed how good the partnership between Fowler and Collymore could be when both were on form, but Collymore had been so inconsistent throughout 1996/97 that he'd often found himself on the bench. In this match, he often picked the ball up in deeper positions before running at the defence and looking to play in the young Toxteth-born striker. It was a formula that had worked throughout the previous season, and it certainly worked here.

Three days later, on 17 December, the formula once again proved fruitful, as Collymore scored two and Fowler scored one as Liverpool beat a Nottingham Forest team sitting bottom of the table 4-2. The win sent Liverpool top of the table by two points, but they now had Arsenal and surprise challengers Wimbledon behind them with a match in hand and two and three points away respectively. If you're wondering … at this point Manchester United were in sixth place, and nine points back.

Liverpool next travelled to the North-east to face Newcastle United on 23 December on *Monday Night Football*. Collymore retained his place, partnering Robbie Fowler up front. The Reds were held to a 1-1 draw on Tyneside, with Fowler scoring just before half-time to cancel out Alan Shearer's 28th-minute tap-in following a David Ginola corner. Fowler was less of an influence overall than he normally would be, following a knock that had forced him off in the latter stages of the win against Forest. The Reds then drew again on Boxing Day, held 1-1 by Leicester City, with a late goal by Collymore sparing their blushes at Anfield, as they looked neutered in attack without Fowler's presence. They then closed out the year with a 1-0 win away at The Dell against Graeme Souness's struggling Southampton, when John Barnes managed to score from around 40 yards after a poor clearance from Saints keeper Dave Beasant left an open goal for the former winger to shoot at. The match also marked Barnes's 300th league appearance for Liverpool.

The victory meant that Liverpool ended 1996 top of the Premier League by five points from a now recovering Manchester United, with Arsenal and Wimbledon also on 37 points. Despite that, Liverpool had shown plenty of inconsistency and still seemed extremely reliant on Steve McManaman for creativity and Robbie Fowler for goals. However, they'd been able to turn poor performances into wins, one of the characteristics of a title-winning team. It seemed most likely that the team that would win the 1996/97 Premier League would be the one to go on a consistent run of form and avoid unnecessary dropped points. As 1997 began, the bookies made Liverpool 13/8 favourites to lift the title for the first time since 1989/90. Spicy.

Unfortunately, Liverpool began 1997 with a loss on a freezing cold New Year's Day as they travelled to London to face Chelsea. Roberto Di Matteo – part of the new influx of foreign talent into the Premier League – gave Ruud Gullit's team the points following some sloppy passing at the back from Liverpool that gifted the ball to him just outside the box with only James to beat. Liverpool had seen plenty of the possession but failed to create any clear-cut chances, with their defeat blowing the title race wide open.

They were in action in both the FA and Coca-Cola Cups over the next few days, beating Burnley 1-0 – with

David James not even having to make a save – at Anfield in the FA Cup third round on 4 January, but crashing out of the Coca-Cola Cup against the inconsistent Middlesbrough on 8 January, losing 2-1 at the Riverside. By the end of January, and a 4-2 defeat by Chelsea on 26 January after leading 2-0, Liverpool were out of the domestic cups for the season.

Back in the Premier League, the Reds hosted West Ham United on 11 January and, despite hitting the woodwork three times in the first half, were admittedly lucky to escape with a 0-0 draw, with David James having plenty to do in the Liverpool goal. The two dropped points were even more significant as both Arsenal and Newcastle United – who had just suffered the resignation of Kevin Keegan and would soon welcome Kenny Dalglish to Tyneside – both dropped points. In addition, Manchester United won against Tottenham, so now were only two points behind Liverpool, with a match in hand. Once again, it was becoming clear that the title was there for the winning, but Evans's team needed to grab the moment with both hands.

The West Ham match had also made Roy Evans's life more difficult as Mark Wright was unavailable through illness, then Neil Ruddock and Phil Babb were forced off with injuries. Fortunately, the day before, Liverpool had secured the signing of Norwegian defender Bjørn Tore Kvarme on a free transfer from Rosenborg, and he went straight into the starting line-up in their final league match of January, in which they soundly beat Aston Villa 3-0 at Anfield, with Jamie Carragher scoring his first goal for the club, playing alongside Jamie Redknapp in central midfield. Their other two goals were scored by Stan Collymore and the ever-present Robbie Fowler. The match also marked Jamie Redknapp's return to the starting line-up. He'd suffered with injuries during the first half of the season and had lost his place to Michael Thomas, who was preferred as his holding role allowed John Barnes to move forward into attack more frequently. However, Redknapp would find himself in Roy Evans's plans more often in the second half of the season, as he continued to rotate with Thomas. As January 1997 ended, Liverpool had dropped to third in the table, with both Manchester United and Arsenal converting their precious matches in hand into points, meaning Liverpool were now one point off the top.

In February, Liverpool found themselves with only the league to focus on, as the Cup Winners' Cup didn't recommence until March. They opened the month at the Baseball Ground as they faced a Derby County team battling for survival. Unfortunately for the Midlands side, Stan Collymore, continuing to keep Patrik Berger out of the team, scored the only goal when he pirouetted wonderfully in the box after receiving the ball from Robbie Fowler and fired a low shot into the bottom corner with his left foot. Collymore was then in form once again as Liverpool demolished Leeds United 4-0 at

Anfield. He set up the first for Robbie Fowler, drilling a wonderful ball across the goal from the byline that left Fowler with nothing else to do but tap it into the empty net. Collymore scored the second, being neatly played in by John Barnes before guiding the ball past keeper Nigel Martyn with his left foot. Liverpool's third again came through Collymore, tapping in a wonderful cross by McManaman as Leeds struggled to cope with the movement of the front three. Jamie Redknapp added a fourth late on with a quick free kick that he sent flying into the top corner from around 25 yards as Leeds took too long in setting up their wall.

Liverpool ended the month unbeaten in the league following an infuriating 0-0 draw at home to Blackburn in which they created plenty of chances but simply failed to put any of them away. Robbie Fowler in particular missed several that were beyond uncharacteristic for a finisher of his quality. Luckily, Manchester United were also held to a draw, meaning February ended with Liverpool only one point behind Sir Alex Ferguson's team and in a genuine title race.

March saw Liverpool back in action in European competition, but the month began with disappointment in the league when they again failed to convert their chances, this time against Aston Villa, and they were sorely punished for it when Ian Taylor scored a late goal that saw Evans's men drop four points behind Manchester United at the top of the table. Four days later, the Reds travelled to Norway to face Brann in the Cup Winners' Cup third round, leaving Scandinavia having laboured to a 1-1 draw. The scoring was opened after a wonderful piece of play by Robbie Fowler, as he controlled a headed pass from Stig Inge Bjørnebye with the outside of his foot, flicking the ball up and over the head of the challenging defender, before running after the ball and firing it past the Brann goalkeeper first time with his left foot. His finishing had been inconsistent in recent matches, but this was an emphatic example of the genius that he was capable of, and why he was the club's most important player by some distance. Unfortunately, Brann equalised just after half-time, capitalising on some sloppy defending from the back three to score through Geir Hasund.

The match saw the return of Patrik Berger to the team, with Collymore dropping to the bench. Berger was used in a role that perhaps suited him more than centre-forward, used primarily to link midfield to attack, with Fowler playing more as a lone striker. He then retained his place for Liverpool's next fixture, as Kenny Dalglish's Newcastle United travelled south to Anfield. The match proved to be another goal-fest, perhaps not quite on the level of the previous season's all-time classic. Crucially, Manchester United had just lost to Sunderland on 8 March, meaning a win would bring Liverpool back within a point of the reigning champions.

Newcastle were without Alan Shearer (groin injury), while Les Ferdinand (hamstring injury) only made the bench, meaning this was a different Newcastle to the one that Liverpool had faced in the famous 4-3 the previous year, and even in the first fixture earlier in the season. The Reds started brightly, with Berger doing a lot of early running to link the midfield to the attack, and the team as a whole were confident enough to pass around Newcastle, who seemed to be chasing the ball constantly. It took until the 29th minute for Liverpool to get the breakthrough, though, as Jamie Redknapp fired a wonderful pass out to the right flank for Jason McAteer to attack. He controlled the ball perfectly and crossed, only for Robbie Fowler to dummy and leave the ball to run on to Steve McManaman, who controlled it and curled his shot wonderfully into the top corner. With the deadlock broken, the floodgates opened and, two minutes later, Patrik Berger gave Liverpool a two-goal lead, tapping into an empty net after Robbie Fowler was unlucky to hit the post after more wonderful play by McManaman. At this point, Liverpool had complete control and were simply passing the ball from red shirt to red shirt, irrespective of whether there were any black-and-white shirts on the pitch. They were then arguably robbed of a penalty when Phillipe Albert used his hand to tackle Patrik Berger well within Newcastle's box, but minutes later Robbie Fowler made it 3-0 after he broke through Newcastle's back line and ran on to a wonderful through ball from Jamie Redknapp – who seemed to be everywhere in the first half – and finished as only Fowler could. As the whistle went to signal half-time, a roar went up around Anfield, followed by applause. However, more was to come.

Kenny Dalglish brought on both Les Ferdinand and David Ginola, with Peter Beardsley and Lee Clark making way at half-time. Unfortunately for Ferdinand, he was only on the Anfield turf for ten minutes before it was clear that he wasn't fit enough and was replaced. Liverpool continue to push and dominate the match, McAteer almost making it four when he fired a shot just wide of the goal after cutting in from the right flank and letting fly from around 20 yards. Later, Newcastle goalkeeper Shaka Hislop was forced into a fine save from a Bjørnebye free kick, as the visitors showed little sign of life. That's until Keith Gillespie scored out of nowhere in the 71st minute, when his shot from outside the box found its way through the hands of David James and squirmed into the bottom corner. Liverpool still had control, although Steve Watson hit the bar following a corner, showing that Newcastle weren't quite done. All of a sudden, some sloppy play in midfield ended up with the ball at the feet of David Ginola, and the Frenchman played the ball long for the onrunning Faustino Asprilla, whose flailing right foot managed to guide the ball up and over David James and into the back of the net. Somehow, having barely been in the match, it was 3-2.

A minute later, Asprilla was influential again, as he controlled a Warren Barton flick-on in the box. The Colombian went down under the pressure of Kvarme's challenge, but the ball fell into the path of Barton, who stabbed it home to equalise, 3-3!

As Roy Evans and his staff looked despondent in the dugout, Newcastle's fans celebrated. They shouldn't have. John Barnes picked the ball up and played it forward to Fowler, who played a first-time pass out to the left flank for Dominic Matteo. Matteo immediately played the ball forward to Bjørnebye, who ran down the flank and crossed. Meanwhile, Robbie Fowler had turned after playing the ball out wide and made his way towards the box, picking up the pace of his run as the cross came in. Wonderfully, amazingly, the cross and Fowler found each other in the crowded penalty box, and Liverpool's No. 9 headed down into the bottom corner and past Hislop to make it 4-3 and to give Liverpool the win they so badly needed in the title race. As Anfield erupted at the final whistle, the Reds were now one point off the top of the table and still had to face Manchester United in April. It had been another crazy 4-3 between Liverpool and Newcastle United, and the Reds had once again come away the winners with a late goal. Evans and his team may have had their issues, but it was moments like this that caused so many to remember this team fondly, and the kind of moments and performances that had been long lost under his predecessor Graeme Souness.

Liverpool could hopefully now take this momentum into the remainder of the season.

Fowler was on the scoresheet again in Liverpool's next league match, as they travelled to the City Ground to face Nottingham Forest five days later. He fired a Jason McAteer cutback into the bottom corner with his weaker right foot to give Liverpool the lead within the first five minutes. However, they were held to a 1-1 draw when David James failed to claim a cross that he had no business coming out for, leaving him scrambling towards his own goal but not in time to stop Ian Woan's shot from the edge of the box. Once again, it was the kind of bizarre decision-making that James was capable of, made even more crucial by the fact that Manchester United won against Sheffield Wednesday. Now Liverpool would need to avoid dropping points to have any chance of competing with United during the run-in.

The Reds now had a welcome break in between league fixtures, as they entertained Brann at a sold-out Anfield for the second leg of their Cup Winners' Cup tie, which stood finely poised after the 1-1 draw in the first leg. Steve Harkness replaced the cup-tied Bjørn Tore Kvarme in the back three, but other than that it was a consistent XI chosen by Roy Evans. Liverpool missed chances early on – Berger basically passing up an open goal by completely miskicking the ball – but they eventually took the lead on the night and on aggregate when Robbie Fowler was brought down clumsily in the box and calmly got up to roll the penalty into the net, sending the Brann goalkeeper the wrong way. Just after half-time, Stan Collymore came on for Patrik Berger, as Liverpool looked to finish the tie off, and the substitution paid dividends as he picked the ball up in midfield, dribbled through the Brann defence, and then was lucky enough to have the ball ricochet off him as a defender scrambled to tackle him. Robbie Fowler made it 4-1 on aggregate with around ten minutes to go, converting Stig Inge Bjørnebye's cutback from the byline into the bottom corner. The victory meant that the Reds had qualified for a European semi-final for the first time since 1985, and Collymore marked the moment by throwing his shirt into the Kop as Anfield celebrated the club's return to European relevance.

Liverpool ended March 1997 with a tough trip to London to face Arsène Wenger's Arsenal, who were level on points with Roy Evans's team, albeit with Liverpool having a match in hand. It was if not a must-win match, then certainly a must-not lose, in order to keep pace with Manchester United at the top. Collymore returned to the starting line-up to partner Robbie Fowler, and it was Collymore who gave the Reds the lead early in the second half, being first to the rebound after Stig Inge Bjørnebye's shot was only parried by David Seaman. Collymore's finishing on the night had been inconsistent at best, but he was a constant threat to Arsenal with his movement and aggressive running. Fifteen minutes later it was a rebound that gave Liverpool their second goal, as Seaman saved a penalty from Robbie Fowler directly into the path of the switched-on Jason McAteer, who beat everyone else to the ball to finish. Ian Wright scored a late goal to make the game look more competitive, but Mark Wright continued to marshal the back three expertly, meaning Liverpool made the journey back north with a hard-earned and vital win. It also meant that they would go into the final month – and a bit – of the Premier League season only three points off the top, and still to play the leaders at Anfield.

Liverpool's first match in April was in the league against Coventry City at Anfield. They were made to wait until the second half to take the lead, doing so through Robbie Fowler, who ran on to a John Barnes through ball to fire a first-time shot with his right foot straight past the Coventry keeper Steve Ogrizovic. Unfortunately, that would be as good as it got for Liverpool, with Fowler, Collymore and McManaman all missing chances, and Coventry drawing level through Noel Whelan in the 65th minute after he met a flick-on from a corner to tap in. Dion Dublin then give Coventry the win in added time after David James made another blunder at a crucial time, coming out to claim a Gary McAllister corner and completely missing it, leaving Dublin to stab the ball in from the goal line. Although James received a large amount of the blame – understandably having committed such an error – Liverpool had been the better team throughout, and the result should really have been well out of sight. Fortunately for them, Manchester United also lost that weekend, to mid-table Derby County. The real winners of the weekend were Arsenal, who moved into second, level on points with the Reds, who were behind them on goal difference but still with a match in hand.

Before the culmination of the Premier League season, however, Liverpool faced the small challenge of their first European semi-final for over a decade at the Parc des Princes against Paris Saint-Germain (PSG). Stan Collymore was selected to partner Robbie Fowler in attack, but it would be at the back – and particularly in goal – where Liverpool had most trouble across the Channel. David James conceded two first-half goals that he really should have done better with, the first a failed punch that left him flailing around in the middle of the box as Leonardo tapped in at the back post. The second was another soft punch from a PSG cross that fell at French feet, leading to a tap-in by Benoît Cauet to make it 2-0. A third goal in the second half gave the reigning champions PSG a three-goal cushion to take to Anfield, and Roy Evans admitted that it was possibly his team's worst performance of the season. It was clear that, after a long and gruelling season, Liverpool's form and performances were beginning to rapidly nosedive.

Fortunately for Evans's team, they faced relegation battlers Sunderland three days later in the league. The match may have been at Roker Park rather than Anfield, but it was certainly a more welcome opponent than any of the top teams would have been following the drubbing in France. Robbie Fowler started on his own up front, with Collymore ruled out due to a hamstring injury, and a certain Michael Owen, named on the team sheet for the first time, on the bench. Owen had signed a professional contract with the club not long after his 17th birthday back in December 1996, and he would go on to become one of the world's most lethal finishers over the next five years. However, it was the incumbent striker Robbie Fowler who gave Liverpool the lead, nodding in an easy header after 33 minutes. They'd been far better in the first half and looked somewhere close to their usual standard. Fowler created their second just into the second half, as he chased a Steve Harkness long ball down the left flank, before crossing low for Steve McManaman to finish calmly inside the penalty box. Sunderland got a goal back only minutes later through former Liverpool man Paul Stewart, but the Reds held on for victory in a match that really was a test of character, given the previous two performances. The victory kept Liverpool within touching distance of the lead, three points back and still to play United.

Three days later, Liverpool travelled to Goodison Park for the second Merseyside derby of the season.

Evans maintained faith in Fowler up front on his own, with both Collymore and Berger on the bench. Although Liverpool, with Sir Alex Ferguson watching from the stands, took the lead midway through the first half after what was eventually ruled an own goal by Claus Thomsen, Duncan Ferguson equalised for Everton with a wonderful turn and shot from just outside the box in the 65th minute. Robbie Fowler was unlucky to hit the post late on, but as tempers flared and Liverpool continued to push forward, Fowler got himself sent off after a battle with David Unsworth that had been going on throughout turned violent after Fowler reacted to an Unsworth tackle by grabbing the Everton defender by the neck. Unsworth also received his marching orders from official Stephen Lodge, but Fowler made matters worse by swinging his arm at Unsworth as he walked off the pitch – and had to be shepherded away by Ronnie Moran and the Liverpool staff.

Fowler would receive a ban for violent conduct and missed the rest of the season after Liverpool's next match. He'd been the club's only reliable striker, with Berger having cooled off since the beginning of the season, and Collymore's form consistently inconsistent, so Liverpool would be without him at a point where they needed to win every available match to have any chance of winning the Premier League title. Their four remaining matches included Tottenham, Wimbledon and Sheffield Wednesday, but first they would host Manchester United at Anfield in a must-win match.

Unfortunately, Fowler's presence could do nothing at Anfield, as Liverpool succumbed to a 3-1 defeat that saw David Beckham provide two first-half goals from the corner flag, as his deliveries repeatedly had David James and his defence bamboozled. John Barnes scored following a Liverpool corner to keep the Reds close at half-time at 2-1, but Andy Cole scored Manchester United's third in the second half when James failed to claim a looping Gary Neville cross, leaving the former Newcastle striker to nod in at the back post. It was another mistake by James in a shocking run of form that had cost his team several times. Questions would surely have to be asked at the end of the season about his future as the club's No. 1. David Beckham completed his masterclass of dead-ball play by almost sending a free kick into the top corner from 25 yards, but as the full-time whistle went, it was clear from the atmosphere around a deflated Anfield that Liverpool's title challenge, which for so long had seen them right at the very top of the table and at one point considered favourites, was well and truly over. They were now five points back from United and the reigning champions had a match in hand.

Five days later, 24 April, saw PSG arrive on Merseyside for the second leg of the Cup Winners' Cup semi-final, with Roy Evans's team having a mountain to climb following the 3-0 collapse in France. He made a significant tactical change for the match, moving to a 4-4-2 that saw Robbie Fowler partnered up front by Stan Collymore, with Patrik Berger playing on the left wing and Steve McManaman shifted out to the right flank. Collymore proved influential in the early stages, setting up Fowler's 11th-minute goal, chasing down a long ball to control it and lay it off to Fowler, whose first-time shot nestled nicely in the bottom corner. Liverpool continued to push throughout and, although PSG often looked nervy and anxious, the second goal didn't arrive until the 79th minute, and it came from an unlikely source. Mark Wright – often Liverpool's only truly reliable defender – fired in a header from a Stig Inge Bjørnebye corner in front of the Kop as Anfield erupted. The Reds now pushed and pushed, but they weren't able to create a chance good enough to level the tie on aggregate, meaning it ended 3-2. Liverpool were out, but, as defeats go, it was one of the more heroic ones the club had suffered lately and really suggested more about what the team were capable of. The previous evening, Manchester United had been defeated by Borussia Dortmund in the semi-finals of the Champions League. It was hard to ignore the fact that English teams were returning to European relevance after several years of being noticeably behind the times tactically.

As April turned to May, Liverpool had three matches remaining and, admittedly, while still technically in the title race, didn't have too much more to play for. The first was at Anfield against Tottenham, where Roy Evans stuck with the 4-4-2 system that had proved so effective against PSG. The Reds won 2-1, with goals from Stan Collymore and Patrik Berger giving them a comeback win after Darren Anderton had given Spurs the lead after five minutes. After the match, Evans admitted that they would continue to work on the 4-4-2 and might use it next season. The 3-5-2 system had become synonymous with Liverpool's play at this point, but there were times when it was clear that Steve McManaman had become Liverpool's lone source of creativity in the final third and more attacking bodies were needed to give McManaman support. Whether Evans would truly make the switch in 1997/98 remained to be seen. Manchester United drew with Leicester City on the same matchday, so Liverpool closed to within three points and represented the only real hope that Sir Alex Ferguson's team could be knocked off the top of the table.

Infuriatingly, a poor Liverpool went on to pick up only one point from their remaining two matches. They suffered defeat at Selhurst Park – returning to the 3-5-2 – against Wimbledon, going 2-0 down thanks to Jason Euell and Dean Holdsworth before Michael Owen came on to at least give the travelling Reds something to cheer. The lightning-quick young striker used his pace to beat the offside trap, before opening up his body in the box and shooting around the goalkeeper and across the goal with his right foot. It was the kind of finish we would see again and again from Owen in the coming years, but this was the original, his first in the famous red shirt. Nevertheless, the defeat handed the title to Manchester United. When Liverpool drew 1-1 with Sheffield Wednesday on the final day, and both Arsenal and Newcastle United recorded emphatic wins, both leapfrogged Liverpool, meaning a season that had promised so much and delivered so much for the first three-quarters of it, ended with Liverpool fourth in the table, missing out on a place in the Champions League for 1997/98. Although they had only themselves to blame for performances at the end of the season, there had been bad luck with injuries to Berger and Collymore, as well as the self-inflicted suspension of Robbie Fowler.

In the end, Liverpool finished 1996/97 with a lingering feeling of disappointment about what could have been. Of all the seasons where they legitimately could have won the title in the mid-1990s, this was the one. During the early portion of the season they'd been top of the table on several occasions, possessed the league's third-top goalscorer in Robbie Fowler and had two players, Steve McManaman and Stig Inge Bjørnebye, named in the PFA Team of the Year. So, what had gone wrong? Liverpool's defence has often been called into question, but they conceded only 37 goals in 1996/97, seven fewer than the league champions and good enough for the third-best record in the league. Sure, the defence had at times been suspect, and David James admittedly had made some poor errors at critical times, which had cost points in the final portion of the season, but it was in attack that Liverpool had fallen behind the leaders, scoring 62 goals, whereas Manchester United scored 76, and second-placed Newcastle United scored 73. Robbie Fowler continued to be prolific, a deadly threat up front and one of the best pure finishers that British football has ever seen, but he'd lacked goalscoring support at crucial times. Collymore had scored 12 here and there, but Berger had only netted six. Still, the team had made progress. Roy Evans had certainly helped the club recover, far exceeding what his predecessor Graeme Souness had been able to do as manager, but now they were in danger of plateauing if they were unable to learn the lessons of 1996/97. More spice perhaps?

Chapter 7

Wannabe – Owen, Ince and 97/98

AFTER LIVERPOOL'S early title challenge eventually fell away in the 1996/97 Premier League season, they entered the summer of 1997 with some important decisions to make. It was clear at the end of the season that they weren't quite at the standard of Manchester United, while Arsène Wenger's Arsenal were rapidly improving and would continue to do so, having signed star winger Marc Overmars from Ajax and midfielder Emmanuel Petit from Monaco in the summer transfer window. It had become increasingly clear that Robbie Fowler desperately needed help up front, and couldn't be the only prolific striker at the club. In addition, the midfield still lacked steel, while the 3-5-2 that had spurred Liverpool's revival post-Souness was now being questioned by Evans himself, with a long-term move to 4-4-2 looking on the cards. On the bright side,

Liverpool still had two of the best players in the Premier League in Robbie Fowler and Steve McManaman, and one of the best left-backs in Stig Inge Bjørnebye. The lingering feeling for the Reds was that the promise that Evans's young team had shown back in 1994/95 now needed to bear fruit, otherwise they faced the permanent frustration of being best of the rest behind Manchester United and Arsenal. Change was needed prior to the start of the 1997/98 season.

That change came quickly, as only two days after the 1996/97 season had ended, Roy Evans and his staff decided enough was enough and allowed Stan Collymore to leave the club, as he headed to the Midlands, joining Aston Villa for a fee of £7m. Collymore had been a key part of Liverpool's excellent 1995/96 and had formed a great partnership with Robbie Fowler, but had been inconsistent throughout 1996/97 and at times had become somewhat of a distraction, missing training and complaining to Evans about being asked to play in the reserves.

He'd also struggled to be part of the core social group at Melwood, his long commute – and late arrivals – to training contributing significantly to that. Collymore remains one of the most naturally gifted English players of the 1990s, and conversations about his talent will always lead to 'what if' scenarios. Despite that, in 1995/96, it has to be said that he more than sacrificed his own game to benefit Robbie Fowler, and the pair flourished together as Liverpool's football captured the hearts of neutrals across the country.

Also leaving in the summer was Michael Stensgaard, the often injured goalkeeper who looked to revive his career back in Denmark with FC København. However, the most emotional departure was that of club captain John Barnes, who was given a free transfer in August 1997, a decade after his £2m move from Watford. Barnes would go on to reunite with former manager Kenny Dalglish at Newcastle as the Scot also brought in Ian Rush and Stuart Pearce, severely ageing Kevin Keegan's entertainers. Barnes had been part of the great Liverpool team of the late-80s with Aldridge, Beardsley and Rush and will rightly go down as an Anfield legend. For several seasons, there was a genuine case to be made that Barnes was the best winger in the world. He'd adapted his game upon the arrival of Roy Evans after a difficult period under Graeme Souness, and had been a valued member of the midfield. Unfortunately for Barnes, it was clear that Evans had a desire to change Liverpool's balance in central midfield, and his departure would be a part of that. Barnes would play with Newcastle until 1999, before joining Charlton Athletic, then retiring as a player.

Arriving at Anfield were several big names, perhaps none bigger than England international Paul Ince, who arrived from Inter Milan. He'd enjoyed two years of individual success in Serie A – the league being perhaps the ultimate measuring stick for individual talent throughout the 1990s – before returning home to England for family reasons. When Sir Alex Ferguson turned down Manchester United's first option to buy back Ince, Roy Evans and Liverpool swept in, signing the all-round central-midfielder for £4.2m. He'd starred in a ball-winning role for England in Euro 96 alongside Paul Gascoigne, and it was hoped he would bring a similar approach to Liverpool's often-criticised midfield. Although many on Merseyside questioned the signing of Ince due to his strong links with Manchester United, as the new club captain he would go on to be ever-present in 1997/98, with only Steve McManaman and a teenage Michael Owen making more appearances in the famous red shirt.

Also joining the Reds was Norwegian winger Øyvind Leonhardsen, who arrived from Joe Kinnear's Wimbledon for £3.5m. Leonhardsen was a talented wide player who had been voted player of the year at Wimbledon on two occasions, and this further signalled a desire by Evans to move away from the 3-5-2 shape. Another name who would become a mainstay at Anfield for years to come was Danny Murphy, who arrived from Crewe Alexandra for £1.5m. Murphy would struggle to make his mark on Merseyside at first, before becoming a key feature of Gérard Houllier's Liverpool team of the early 2000s.

But perhaps one of the most interesting signings in the entirety of Evans's tenure as manager was the

£1.5m purchase of Karl-Heinz Riedle from Borussia Dortmund. Riedle had actually started the previous season's Champions League Final for Dortmund against Marcello Lippi's great Juventus team, scoring two goals. Concerningly for those who looked deeper at this signing, Riedle hadn't bagged double-digit goals in the Bundesliga since his return to Germany from Lazio in 1993. However, Riedle was a signing in a clear area of need, giving Robbie Fowler much-needed goalscoring support like he'd received from Ian Rush at the beginning of his career. Evans and Liverpool weren't to know that another striker at Anfield would explode on to the scene, in a way that no teenager had before.

Liverpool began the season away from home, travelling south to play Wimbledon at Selhurst Park. They began the season still in their 3-5-2 system, with Karl-Heinz Riedle partnering young Michael Owen up front, with Robbie Fowler out injured. In fact, it would be a season of injury for Fowler that would eventually see him miss out on the 1998 World Cup. Paul Ince also made his debut for the Reds, partnering Michael Thomas in a much more functional midfield two behind Steve McManaman in his patented floating role behind the strikers. The match was notable for Michael Owen opening his account for the season, scoring from a penalty to bring the scores level after Marcus Gayle had scored for Wimbledon. However, Liverpool were held to a 1-1 draw and Neil Ruddock suffered a knee injury that would see him out for the next two months. Also of note was the Liverpool debut of Danny Murphy, replacing Bjørnebye in the second half.

Four days later, Liverpool played their first match of the season at Anfield, hosting Leicester City. Evans stuck with 3-5-2, with Steve Harkness replacing Ruddock at the back. Unfortunately, it was yet more frustration for Liverpool, as they conceded a goal courtesy of Matt Elliot in the first minute, when he stabbed in at the back post, beating Phil Babb, who really should have done better. Evans moved the formation away from the 3-5-2 after the break, as Murphy replaced Bjørnebye again, but it wouldn't make much difference, as Leicester scored a second late on when David James palmed an Emile Heskey shot directly into the path of the on-running Graham Fenton. Paul Ince showed his class and leadership by smashing in a shot from 25 yards a few minutes later before passionately telling his players to get back to the centre-circle, but the late revival wasn't enough as the score remained 2-1, the Reds deserving little more thanks to their shocking performance.

They were poor again when they travelled to Ewood Park to face Roy Hodgson's Blackburn Rovers later in the month, with Evans again sticking with the 3-5-2. Liverpool actually took the lead when Michael Owen scored his second of the season, capitalising on a loose pass around the Blackburn defence and using his incredible pace to run beyond the scrambling

Blackburn back line, finishing past John Filan. It was an example of the kind of natural talent that Owen possessed, as well as the ability to coolly finish when in tight spaces. Annoyingly for Owen, Evans and all in red on Merseyside, a late equaliser from Martin Dahlin rescued a draw for Blackburn, who at that point were top of the table. In stark and shocking contrast, Liverpool were 15th.

The Reds badly needed to get their act together. Thankfully, they ended August by recording their first victory of the season when they won 2-0 at Elland Road against Leeds United, with Steve McManaman scoring the first when he dribbled at the Leeds defence from the right flank before firing a hard shot across Nigel Martyn. Their second goal on the night was a delightful first club goal from Karl-Heinz Riedle, as he elegantly chipped the keeper from just outside the box, floating the ball into the far corner as Martyn flailed after it. The win sent Evans's team hurtling up the table to eighth.

September 1997 saw a return to form, as the Reds lost only once in the league all month. Roy Evans named an unchanged line-up – interestingly with Rob Jones now starting at right wing-back in place of Jason McAteer – as Sheffield Wednesday travelled to Anfield. Liverpool's central midfield was responsible for the win, as captain Paul Ince opened the scoring after a goalmouth scramble in the 55th minute, before Michael Thomas made it two in the 68th, firing in a left-footed shot from the edge of the box into the far corner. Wednesday scored in the 80th minute to make things more interesting in the final ten minutes, but Liverpool held on, despite a relatively average performance. With Robbie Fowler due to return later in the month, questions began to be asked about how he would fit back into the team, with Michael Owen showing some form to begin the campaign, in contrast to Karl-Heinz Riedle, who had contributed little despite his goal at Elland Road.

Three days later, on 16 September, Liverpool began their European campaign for the season as they travelled beyond Hadrian's Wall to face Celtic in the UEFA Cup. Liverpool were virtually unchanged and started brightly at Celtic Park, going 1-0 up within the first seven minutes thanks to Michael Owen, who received the ball following some nice passing on the left flank, before accelerating away from the Celtic defence and neatly lifting the ball over Jonathan Gould in goal. The Reds continued to press forward and looked as if they'd easily come away with a victory, but as the match went on, their standard dropped as Celtic continued to work and grind away. They drew level early in the second half when Dominic Matteo failed to deal with a through ball and inadvertently guided it into the path of Jackie McNamara, who finished past David James. Then 20 minutes later Celtic attacked again and won themselves a penalty when Henrik Larsson just beat James to a ball behind the Liverpool defence and went down after some rather minimal contact. Simon Donnelly smashed the ball in from the penalty spot and somehow Celtic now had a 2-1 lead. Liverpool were saved eventually by some individual class, as Steve McManaman picked the ball up in the right-back position and controlled it past a Celtic player, before driving infield at pace, unchallenged by anyone in a green-and-white hooped shirt, then firing a shot with his left foot into the bottom corner of the net as he arrived the box. In the end, Liverpool made the journey south with a draw, when they really should have had the match won in the first half.

Returning to domestic action four days later, the Reds journeyed down to the south coast to face Southampton at The Dell. Despite Karl-Heinz Riedle scoring his second goal for the club late in the first half, Liverpool were held to a draw by David Jones's team – their now former manager Graeme Souness having resigned in the summer – after Kevin Davies scored in the 48th minute. As Liverpool were held to a draw yet again, they were in seventh place, six points behind early leaders Arsenal, with a match in hand. They certainly weren't out of the title race but they needed to pick up wins more consistently and avoid dropping points against teams they really should have been beating, like Southampton. Hopefully, the return of Robbie Fowler, who came on for Michael Owen in the 60th minute against the Saints, would get the Reds firing again.

Evans's team was back in league action just two days later, as they welcomed Aston Villa to Anfield. The match saw a switch from 3-5-2 to 4-4-2, as Bjørn Tore Kvarme was selected at right-back, and Phil Babb was partnered in central defence by Jamie Carragher. Stig Inge Bjørnebye retained his place on Liverpool's left side, but as a left-back rather than left wing-back. Steve McManaman returned to the spot on the right wing that he'd occupied in his early days under Graeme Souness, while Danny Murphy partnered Michael Thomas in central midfield and Patrik Berger was selected on the left flank. Up front, Liverpool's two lethal strikers were given the chance to play together as Robbie Fowler and Michael Owen were selected to start. The 3-5-2 had been such a core part of Liverpool's improvement under Evans, but it had become clear towards the end of 1996/97 and at the beginning of 1997/98 that something needed to change to make the team less reliant on Fowler and McManaman.

They hardly looked prolific in the 4-4-2, but three second-half goals from Robbie Fowler, Steve McManaman and Karl-Heinz Riedle – a goal delightfully created by a mazy dribble from Owen through the Villa defence – gave the Reds the points. Unfortunately, they then lost their next league fixture at Upton Park, despite the return of captain Paul Ince, beaten 2-1 by West Ham. The lone bright spot was a glorious volley scored by Robbie Fowler, taking the ball first time with his gifted left foot from 20 yards out. The loss left Liverpool in a distant ninth position at the end of September, already seven points behind Arsenal.

September ended with the hosting of European football at Anfield, as the Reds welcomed Celtic to the famous ground for the second leg of their UEFA Cup tie. Evans continued with the 4-4-2, shifting Jamie Carragher into central midfield alongside Ince, meaning that Kvarme and Babb were the choice in central defence, while Rob Jones returned at right-back. Evans hoped that Fowler and Owen could work together up front, with the younger of the two undroppable at that time, despite the signing of Riedle to provide support for Fowler. Liverpool eventually managed to make it through the tie, with the match ending 0-0, meaning an away-goals win, but they hadn't performed well as their season continued to stutter and stumble.

October began at Anfield, with a game against Ruud Gullit's Chelsea. For this match, Michael Owen made way, replaced by Karl-Heinz Riedle to play alongside Robbie Fowler. However, it was another of Liverpool's strikers who received all the plaudits on the day, as Patrik Berger scored his first hat-trick for the club in a 4-2 victory – Fowler bagging Liverpool's fourth – that meant they moved up to sixth. Ten days later, following the international break, which saw Ince, McManaman and Fowler in the England squad to face Italy, Liverpool took on West Brom in the Coca-Cola Cup third round and put in one of their best performances of the season, winning 2-0 at The Hawthorns with a near full-strength line-up, only Ince missing due to a head injury suffered in Rome. Patrik Berger scored again, giving Liverpool the lead, before Robbie Fowler made it two in the dying minutes. The cup tie also saw Øyvind Leonhardsen's first appearance in a Liverpool shirt following his £3.5m move from Wimbledon.

Leonhardsen was back on the bench again for Liverpool's next fixture, the first Merseyside derby of the season, at Goodison Park. Roy Evans altered the team slightly, with Paul Ince returning to the line-up, and Jason McAteer and Neil Ruddock making their first appearances for some time. Infuriatingly for the Liverpool manager, his team simply didn't turn up to play, succumbing to a 2-0 defeat that saw them plummet to ninth. In the end, their performance deserved nothing less. Three days later in the UEFA Cup, they lost 3-0 to French team Strasbourg in a sluggish performance that gave the travelling support at Stade de la Meinau absolutely nothing to cheer. What made matters worse was Evans's choice of line-up, with Robbie Fowler his only true striker on the pitch. This time, Liverpool's defence was right to receive much of the blame for their performance.

When Derby County came to Anfield on 25 October, serious questions were starting to be asked about Liverpool's performances. They'd been bad more often than they'd been good since the start of the season and had lost much of the attacking swagger that the club was so renowned for, and that Evans's team in particular had been known for. He returned to the back four system, with Dominic Matteo partnering Bjørn Tore Kvarme, and it yielded a much better performance from the Reds. Robbie Fowler and Michael Owen were a constant threat to the Derby defence – evidence that the pair could play together successfully. Øyvind Leonhardsen also made his first league start for the club, playing on the opposite flank to McManaman in the 4-4-2. Liverpool attacked with fluidity, opening the scoring through Fowler, after some nice interchange found the striker just inside the box, allowing him to fire across the keeper and into the corner. Leonhardsen scored his first goal for the club following some excellent work from Fowler, who dribbled his way around the Derby defence, finding McManaman on the left flank, who laid the ball inside for Leonhardsen to run on to and finish nicely. Captain Ince was to thank for Liverpool's third, as he expertly broke up a Derby attack before releasing McManaman down the left flank; he simply dribbled infield before laying the ball to Fowler in the box, and he did the rest. McManaman capped off a fantastic individual performance by scoring a rare headed goal from a corner in the 88th minute as Liverpool recorded a much-needed 4-0 win, reassuring many on Merseyside that they were still a good team, capable of playing some fantastic football and competing at the top level.

As October ended, Liverpool were sixth in the table, a quite amazing feat considering their dreadful start. They sat seven points away from Manchester United, who had rescued their position at the top, one point ahead of Arsenal. Liverpool still had a match in hand that could bring them closer, but they would certainly need to perform at a high level more consistently to have any chance of interrupting the two-horse race that was developing between United and Arsenal.

November finally saw Liverpool begin to find some proper form, as they lost only once in the entire month. However, they began with a 1-1 draw at the Reebok against Bolton Wanderers, a game which saw both Robbie Fowler and Paul Ince receive suspensions, Ince simply for an accumulation of cards, but Fowler for violent conduct as he lashed out at Bolton's Per Frandsen right in front of the official Dermot Gallagher. Crucially, Fowler's rash judgement would see him ruled out of Liverpool's matches against Barnsley, Arsenal and Manchester United. The dropped points against Bolton saw the Reds fall nine points behind United. Three days later, Liverpool were knocked out of the UEFA Cup by Strasbourg, 3-2 on aggregate, having won the second leg 2-0 and threatening to level the tie, but the rally wasn't enough. Evans was criticised for not putting more strikers on early enough, but in reality it was the shockingly poor performance in France that caused them to drop out of Europe in 1997/98. With their form the way it was, being able to focus solely on domestic matters might not have been the worst thing.

Four days later, Liverpool faced a struggling Tottenham Hotspur, who were 16th in the table, under manager Gerry Francis. It was Robbie Fowler's last appearance in a red shirt for the remainder of the month and Liverpool certainly made the most of it, winning 4-0 at Anfield, with Karl-Heinz Riedle partnering Fowler up front. The Reds looked shaky in defence early on, however, with Kvarme almost gifting Steffen Iversen the opening goal when he passed the ball into Dominic Matteo while trying to play out from the back. Steve McManaman gave Liverpool the lead just after half-time, when he was fortunate enough to be on the receiving end of a tap-in after a shot from Jamie Redknapp was spilled by goalkeeper Ian Walker. Two minutes later they doubled their led as Øyvind Leonhardsen received a rebound from a Robbie Fowler shot and guided the ball into the far corner with his left foot. It was almost three immediately from kick-off but Paul Ince's hard shot was saved by Walker. Liverpool became rampant and almost scored again through Fowler after he was played in by Ince, but his first shot was saved and, although he was first to the rebound, his second shot hit the post from a very narrow angle. Jamie Redknapp did make it three after 65 minutes, with a lovely, guided shot from

20 yards after a lay-off from Fowler, capping off a fine run of form that had seen him return to the starting line-up as Ince's partner in central midfield. Michael Owen scored Liverpool's fourth, and his first at Anfield, in typical fashion, breaking the offside trap to meet an Ince through ball, before sliding in against the keeper and winning it before finishing. It was one of Liverpool's best performances of the season so far, showing that the 4-4-2 was more than suitable as the system, but the niggling question remained as to whether Fowler and Owen could play in it together.

Liverpool's next fixture was in the Coca-Cola Cup fourth round, which saw Owen bag his first hat-trick for the club, as he scythed his way through the Grimsby defence en route to three goals as the Reds won 3-0. Infuriatingly, they then lost 1-0 to Barnsley at Anfield, in a match where Karl-Heinz Riedle had several gilt-edged opportunities to win it, but spurned each one. Barnsley certainly rode their luck but this was a classic example of the way Liverpool had shown themselves capable of dropping points throughout the 1990s, going back to Souness's reign as boss. It was the first time that Barnsley had played Liverpool since 1959 – illustrating the gulf between the two clubs – but it was a famous victory for the Tykes.

Next up for the Reds was a match against Arsenal at Highbury on *Super Sunday*. Arsenal were themselves coming off a poor performance, losing 2-0 to Sheffield

Wednesday, meaning they'd slipped to fourth in the table, four points behind Manchester United, who continued to set the pace at the top. Evans set his team out in the 4-4-2, the only changes being McAteer playing right-back in place of Rob Jones, and Jamie Carragher chosen in central midfield in place of the suspended Paul Ince. Karl-Heinz Riedle continued to be the chosen strike partner up front, this time alongside Michael Owen. Steve McManaman led out the team in what was certainly a must-win match for any title hopes, as pressure built on Roy Evans and rumours swirled about his future come the end of the season.

The first 20 minutes really saw little from either team, with Arsenal the ones who looked capable of breaking through the opposition back four. Liverpool's midfield passing was elegant and attractive but lacked any real penetration, despite the consistent running and effort of Michael Owen. It was Owen who gave Liverpool their first bright moment, picking the ball up in the left half-space just outside the box and driving at the Arsenal back line before cutting the ball back from the byline. Unfortunately, it managed to evade every yellow Liverpool shirt in the box, so Owen's effort went unrewarded. Once again, it showed his natural ability to create something from nothing using his unbelievable turn of pace. After this, the Reds clearly grew in confidence and began to push forward with more regularity, Owen continuing to be a threat with his direct running. Despite a good end to the half from Arsenal, Liverpool's first-half performance was solid, so Roy Evans certainly wouldn't have had any pressing concerns.

The second half picked up with largely the same pattern as the first, Arsenal having the majority of the efforts on goal but none of them really threatening David James, and possession remaining largely equal between both teams at 51:49. It was a moment of pure genius in the 58th minute that broke the deadlock to give Liverpool a 1-0 lead, when Steve McManaman spun away from a Stig Inge Bjørnebye throw from the left wing and hit a first-time shot from just inside the Arsenal box, sending the ball flying across David Seaman and into the far corner. McManaman had worked tirelessly in the midfield and more than deserved the goal for his excellent performance. As the second half continued, Arsenal petered out, with Liverpool becoming increasingly comfortable, Carragher working hard in midfield to repel Arsenal attacks. As the loyal travelling support from Merseyside began to sing, 'You'll Never Walk Alone', Liverpool played out time, winning 1-0 at Highbury, and moving up to seventh in the table, only two points behind Arsenal. However, as November bled into December, they remained nine points behind Manchester United, who looked set to continue building their dynasty.

Liverpool began December by welcoming United to Anfield. The encounter was a disappointment, however, as the in-form Andy Cole scored two, his 11th and 12th in eight matches, to leave Anfield with a 3-1 victory – United's third goal being scored by David Beckham. Cole had been partnered up front by a new signing at Old Trafford in Teddy Sheringham, and he and Cole dovetailed expertly in the United attack. It was noticeable throughout these seasons in the mid- to late-1990s that where Liverpool's recruitment could be labelled average at best, Sir Alex Ferguson and the executives in Manchester almost always got it right. The defeat once again emphasised that United were the dominant team in the country and a gap in quality remained between them and the reds on Merseyside. The loss dropped Liverpool to eighth in the table, with much work left to do to recover their season in the remaining months.

The rest of December 1997 at least saw Liverpool hit a purple patch, winning every remaining match in a run that saw them rocket up to fourth in the table. It began with a 3-0 defeat of Crystal Palace that saw Steve McManaman captain the team in the absence of Paul Ince, and it was he who opened the scoring in the 39th minute, volleying home a Jason McAteer cross from close range. McManaman then began the move that created the second goal, with some lovely interchange in midfield releasing Michael Owen beyond the Palace offside trap, and the young wonderkid deftly lofted the ball over the onrushing Kevin Miller and into the Palace net. Leonhardsen added the third six minutes later.

The run of results continued a week later back at Anfield when Michael Owen scored the only goal in a 1-0 victory over Coventry, where Liverpool at times looked shaky, with David James receiving hefty criticism for his distribution from the back, but they held on regardless. James would soon be under increased pressure for his place following the £1m spent on goalkeeper Brad Friedel from MLS side Columbus Crew. He joined the club just before Christmas Day, after a lengthy battle for a work permit. James had received much of the blame for Liverpool's poor form to end the 1996/97 season and, with the American goalkeeper joining the club, it was clear his place between the sticks was now more at threat than it had been for some time.

On Boxing Day, Friedel was named on the bench as Liverpool hosted Leeds United at Anfield and, with Ince returning, they produced one of their best performances of the season thus far. Fowler and Owen tore the Leeds defence to shreds in a 3-1 win, with Fowler bagging two, and Owen one. The Reds then closed out 1997 by journeying north to Newcastle, coming away from St James' Park with a 2-1 comeback victory following Steve Watson's opener. McManaman was simply brilliant on the night, scoring both goals as Liverpool jumped to fourth. He was rewarded for his sublime performances throughout December with the Premier League Player of the Month award. As 1997 became 1998, Evans's team were still nine points behind Manchester United at the top, but only four behind Blackburn Rovers in second. Suddenly, Liverpool's season looked far from over.

Liverpool began 1998 with an FA Cup third-round tie against Coventry City at Anfield. Unfortunately, the Reds would go no further in the competition following a shocking performance that saw them lose 3-1, despite Roy Evans's selection of a mostly full-strength line-up, featuring McManaman, Ince, Fowler et al. It was once again an example of the kind of poor performances and inconsistency that they'd shown at inconvenient times over the past several years. At least they progressed beyond Newcastle United just days later in the quarter-finals of the Coca-Cola Cup, outlasting the north-east team 2-0 after extra time, to face Middlesbrough in the semis.

Liverpool remained unbeaten in the league throughout the remainder of the month, defeating Wimbledon on 10 January, Jamie Redknapp giving Liverpool the lead with a left-footed strike from just inside the box, and then making it two with a delightful shot from the edge of the box with his stronger right foot that sent the ball flying into the top corner, well out of reach of Neil Sullivan in the Wimbledon goal. The match also saw Phil Babb's first league start since October, returning to the back four following injury. A week later, the Reds dropped points at Filbert Street in a goalless draw against Martin O'Neill's hard-working Leicester City. Then, three days later, they again played

Newcastle, with a glorious first-time shot on the bounce by Michael Owen from the left-hand side of the box providing the only goal in a win that took them up to third in the table, miraculously now only five points behind Manchester United.

The first leg of that Coca-Cola Cup semi-final against Middlesbrough saw the Reds defeat the Teesside outfit 2-1, through goals by Jamie Redknapp and Robbie Fowler. Unfortunately, a goalless draw in the league the following weekend against second-placed Blackburn Rovers saw Liverpool drop to fourth, but United's loss to Leicester meant they were now only four points adrift as the first month of 1998 ended. One can only imagine where Liverpool would have been if had they hit the ground running at the start of the season, as opposed to dropping points in five of their first nine league matches.

At this point, other rumours began to float around Anfield as well. For several years, Liverpool's two best players had undoubtedly been Robbie Fowler and Steve McManaman. The latter had only 18 months left on his contract and was being linked with Spanish giants Barcelona, to the point where Barça's President Joan Gaspart claimed that personal details had already been agreed with the creative midfielder and that he was set to join the Catalan club for £12m. The irony behind this was that Liverpool had agreed a £12.3m deal with Barcelona for McManaman earlier in the season, but the Englishman had failed to agree terms to depart for

Spain. McManaman stated that there was no truth in the claims, but the matter of the midfielder's contract was becoming more and more of a concern for the club, with the Bosman ruling still in its relative infancy and Spanish and Italian clubs circling. Another concern that was picking up steam in the papers was the lack of form of Robbie Fowler, who remained goalless in the league since Boxing Day, and his form wasn't about to improve.

Unfortunately, things wouldn't go well for the Reds as a whole in February, since they failed to record a single victory across both competitions they remained active in. Their first match of the month was at Anfield against Southampton, in which they battered the south coast club but somehow came away with a 3-2 defeat thanks to some poor defending. Both goals for the Reds were scored by Michael Owen, but his second was in the 90th minute as they chased the game following two late goals from Southampton in the 85th and 90th minutes. Incredibly, due to results elsewhere – Tottenham Hotspur beating Blackburn 3-0 – the defeat saw Liverpool up to third on goal difference. A week later, at Hillsborough, Michael Owen scored a wonderful hat-trick that typified his sublime talent. His first was his bread and butter, as he ran on to a through ball from McManaman, beating the offside trap and finishing calmly past the Wednesday keeper. His second was a difficult tap-in past several Wednesday shirts after Robbie Fowler had been unlucky to only hit the post with his right-foot shot. Owen returned to his classic manoeuvre for his third, as he ran beyond the defence to collect Paul Ince's teasing through ball, before guiding the ball into the far corner with the outside of his right foot. It was an example of the effortless natural ability to run beyond slower defenders and finish effortlessly that he seemed to have been born with. His status as the future of the club – and the England team – seemed only too obvious to anyone watching Liverpool in 1997/98. Unfortunately, his goals only bagged a point for the Reds, as they let in three of their own, two of them arguably because of individual mistakes that could have been avoided. Once again, results elsewhere saw Liverpool somehow move up the table, this time to second, although now seven points behind United, after they recorded their first win in three matches by beating Aston Villa 2-0. At this point, the league title once again looked virtually sewn up for the country's most dominant club.

Four days later, Liverpool saw any real hope of silverware for the season end when they lost 2-0 at the Riverside against Bryan Robson's Middlesbrough. Evans chose to rotate somewhat, with Stig Inge Bjørnebye returning for the first time since December and Patrik Berger getting a rare start, his first since November. Evans also set the team out in the 3-5-2, with a back three of Carragher, Matteo and Harkness. Both Middlesbrough goals were scored in a whirlwind first five minutes, firstly by Paul Merson from the penalty spot, then by Marco Branca, running on to a hopeful long ball through the Liverpool back line and finishing well past David James. In the end, the two goals were enough to see Middlesbrough through 3-2 on aggregate and send them to Wembley. After the match, Roy Evans accepted that his defence had largely been the issue and, once again rumours abounded about the manager's future post-1997/98.

There was little time to contemplate that, however, as Liverpool's next league match five days later was the Merseyside derby, a fixture that the Reds hadn't won since March 1994, despite being by far the superior team throughout that period. They returned to the 4-4-2 system, with Carragher continuing in defence alongside Rob Jones, Steve Harkness and Bjørn Tore Kvarme. One of the major weaknesses that continued to persist with their defence was the inconsistency of the back four. Jason McAteer, Phil Babb, Mark Wright, Neil Ruddock, Stig Inge Bjørnebye and Dominic Matteo had all been selected at some point for the back line, and while the previous chapter may have argued that Liverpool's collapse in 1996/97 was due to more than just defensive issues, it's hard to ignore the fact that the back four was a rotating door of centre-backs and full-backs throughout the season.

In front of the back four, the system remained pretty stable, with Ince and Redknapp in central midfield, Leonhardsen and McManaman on the wings – with

McManaman still being given plenty of licence to roam – and Fowler and Owen up front. It was that line-up that faced Howard Kendall's Everton at Anfield. After a scoreless first half, it was Everton who took the lead, with the ultra-physical Duncan Ferguson receiving a knock-down in the Liverpool box and firing into the corner of the goal with his right foot. Liverpool captain Paul Ince brought the Reds level ten minutes later as he pounced on a poorly bundled clearance by the Everton defence and fired into the corner from point-blank range. Although Liverpool avoided defeat, another two points dropped saw them nine points off the top, now in third, with Arsenal rapidly rising up the table in second. In turn, they were nine points behind United but with two matches in hand and still to play the reigning champions. The Merseyside derby also saw Robbie Fowler go off injured in the 90th minute following a collision with Everton keeper Thomas Myhre. The damage would later be revealed to be a devastating anterior cruciate ligament injury that would see the 22-year-old miss the remainder of the season, as well as the 1998 World Cup in France. The injury also left Liverpool with just Karl-Heinz Riedle to partner Michael Owen for the remaining matches.

Liverpool ended February with a 2-1 loss to Aston Villa, leaving them very little chance of returning to the title race they'd seemingly stumbled into in January. Michael Owen opened the scoring in the sixth minute with a well-taken penalty but former Liverpool striker Stan Collymore came back to haunt Roy Evans with two goals to gain himself some revenge, and the Birmingham club the victory. Evans also gave new £1m signing Brad Friedel his first start in the match and he would be the starting goalkeeper for the remainder of the league campaign. The defeat saw Liverpool slip to fourth in the table and at this point it would be tough not to argue that Liverpool's season was effectively over. All that remained was to try to finish as high up the table as possible.

Results would be good for Liverpool during the final months of the league season, losing only twice after their dreadful February. March started with a 2-1 win over struggling Bolton Wanderers at Anfield, as goals from Ince and Owen gave them a comeback win after Alan Thompson had scored within the first ten minutes. Next up was a journey south to London to face a Tottenham team sitting just one place above the relegation zone, Spurs had replaced Gerry Francis with Swiss coach Christian Gross back in November. The match was an end-to-end affair that finished 3-3, with Liverpool breaking Spurs hearts by scrambling in a last-minute equaliser through Steve McManaman after Michael Owen had hit the post. That same matchday, Arsenal helped Liverpool out considerably by beating Manchester United 1-0 at Old Trafford through Marc Overmars, meaning the Reds were nine points behind in third but with a match in hand to bring them closer. However, more significantly, Arsenal were now six points behind the leaders, with a massive three matches in hand.

Two weeks later, at Barnsley, Liverpool continued to ship goals, but fortunately they were able to score three of their own to Barnsley's two, with Karl-Heinz Riedle making two in a poor season, the first a scuffed tap-in, the second a 25-yard strike into the top corner. McManaman scored the winner in the dying minutes, taking control of the ball in the box before deftly chipping the ball over the scrambling goalkeeper. Once again, he'd come up big for Liverpool and he was thanked by a mini pitch invasion from the travelling support at Oakwell.

The Reds then had a 13-day wait until their next fixture, on 10 April. The opponents would be Manchester United, still top of the table, but only six points ahead of Arsenal, who still had their three matches in hand. This was certainly a must-win game for United, who opened the scoring within the first 15 minutes, centre-back Ronny Johnsen powering home a header from a corner. However, Liverpool pegged United back in the 37th minute when Michael Owen chased down a seemingly lost Danny Murphy flick-on – he was partnering the young striker up front – and simply easing past the chasing Gary Pallister to knock the ball beyond Peter Schmeichel and into the goal. Unfortunately, three minutes later Owen received his first and only red card in English football for a second bookable offence, following a late challenge that left United's Johnsen with damaged ankle ligaments. Despite the setback of being down to ten men, Phil Babb and Dominic Matteo continued to marshal the Liverpool back four and, although United had some late chances through Cole and Scholes, the champions never really looked capable of winning. The draw allowed Liverpool to retain a claim to be chasing the title, but the real winners were Arsenal, who were now just four points behind United with those three matches in hand, after their 3-1 home victory over Newcastle, thanks to goals from their mercurial young Frenchman Nicolas Anelka and their midfield machine Patrick Vieira.

Three days later, Liverpool maintained their third place in the table with a 2-1 victory over Crystal Palace at Anfield that did little to thrill spectators, despite a late winner by David Thompson – his first Liverpool goal – grabbing the three points for the Reds. The following weekend, on 19 April, Michael Owen scored his 21st goal of the season to give Liverpool the lead against Coventry City, but Dion Dublin equalised to leave it 1-1. With his performances, Owen was now clearly becoming a legitimate option for England manager Glenn Hoddle ahead of the 1998 World Cup in France, joining fellow Liverpool men Jamie Redknapp and Steve McManaman as potential candidates for the final England squad. Many of the Liverpool squad might have already had the World Cup on their mind, as Liverpool closed out April with a shockingly poor 4-1 loss to Gianluca Vialli's

Chelsea at Stamford Bridge. Post-match, Roy Evans took responsibility for the performance but made a pretty clear statement that some of the squad also needed to take their share of responsibility. There was absolutely no ambiguity when he said that he would get new players if he had to.

Liverpool began May by showing their real quality – which unfortunately they hadn't been able to consistently display – as they dispatched West Ham United 5-0 at Anfield, with Michael Owen simply unplayable, the West Ham defence unable to stop him. Jason McAteer also performed excellently, scoring twice while starting on the right wing in the 4-4-2, a position that suited him far more than right-back had earlier in the season. Owen, Ince and Leonhardsen scored the other three Liverpool goals as they secured European football for the 1998/99 season. Then, incredibly, they welcomed champions elect Arsenal to Anfield on 6 May and emphatically thrashed the Gunners 4-0 through goals from Michael Owen, Øyvind Leonhardsen and a brace from skipper Paul Ince. Once again this demonstrated the undoubted quality that lay at the heart of this Liverpool team – quality that had been there since Evans took over in 1994 – but had been displayed far too infrequently to constitute any real title challenge.

As if to prove the point, they ended their league campaign with a 1-0 defeat at Pride Park by Derby County. It was Liverpool's first defeat against Derby since

SPICE UP YOUR LIFE

1978. They fielded a team missing Ince, McManaman, Leonhardsen and McAteer, but it was still a sluggish performance. Roy Evans's team had gone into the match knowing third place was already sewn up, and it showed.

In the end, Roy Evans's Liverpool finished 1997/98 third in the table, a full 13 points behind champions Arsenal. It had been a disappointing season for the Reds, with inconsistent performances throughout and points dropped at infuriating times. They'd started the season poorly and never really recovered but had displayed the ability to go toe to toe with Manchester United and Arsenal. However, across a 38-match season they'd shown themselves still to be off the pace, and the distance to the two teams above them now looked greater. Questions were being asked about the team's progress. In 1995/96, they were the most entertaining team in the country, playing a distinct brand of football in a system that worked well for the key members of the team. Now that potential appeared to have plateaued, recruitment had been inadequate in comparison to rivals Manchester United and Arsenal, and the football more often looked fragile rather than entertaining. The 3-5-2 had gradually become more negative and had given way to a 4-4-2 that had made little difference. The back four positions had also become a revolving door throughout the season due to injuries and lack of form, and the two constants in the team since Evans's appointment in Robbie Fowler and Steve McManaman were now in a state of flux, Fowler having suffered a career-altering injury, and McManaman yet to sign a new contract and being constantly linked to clubs in Italy and Spain.

Yes, the 'Spice Boys' moniker continued to be thrown at the players by the often overreacting British media of the 1990s, but there were far larger problems facing the club now as the footballing world headed to France for the 1998 World Cup, a tournament that would see Michael Owen become a worldwide star after his wonder goal against Argentina in the knockouts. His breakout remained the lone bright spot from 1997/98 and he was now undoubtedly one of the most talented young players in world football, but back on Merseyside, things would need to improve in 1998/99. The question was: how? Perhaps a more Continental approach?

Chapter 8

Goodbye – Evans to Houllier

AFTER A Premier League campaign in 1997/98 that promised much but failed to deliver any real title challenge, it was clear to all in red on Merseyside that change was required in some way ahead of the next season. A study of the last two seasons since the heyday of Evans's team in 1995/96 had seen stagnation, and much-needed recruitment to improve the squad had been sorely lacking. To put that into perspective, Manchester United had brought in Andy Cole, Ole Gunnar Solskjær, Teddy Sheringham and Ronny Johnsen during this period – all of whom, except for Solskjær, would likely have started for Liverpool. Arsenal had been even more aggressive, bringing in Patrick Vieira, Nicolas Anelka, Marc Overmars and Emmanuel Petit. Again, all of the above would have made it into the Liverpool team. Wherever the issues lay, the club and Evans needed to make changes ahead of 1998/99, as Liverpool risked becoming a team that failed to live up to their potential and becoming relative also-rans in the title race.

Rumours about Roy Evans's job security had been abundant throughout 1997/98. It had been openly discussed on Sky Sports' *Super Sunday* when Liverpool had travelled to London to face Arsenal at Highbury. It was believed that any change would involve Evans being removed from his post as manager and replaced by a suitable alternative. In the end, what the Liverpool board decided to do baffled and confused everyone, Roy Evans included. In July 1998, Liverpool Football Club held a press conference to announce that Gérard Houllier had been appointed to manage the first team, but in a joint-manager role along with Roy Evans. At the press conference for the footballing media, Houllier stated that this decision had only been made with the approval of Roy Evans, who sat beside him, and that he wouldn't have taken the job without this. Houllier talked about the desire to mix his own knowledge with Evans's immense experience and knowledge of the club, and that they would work together, having similar ideas about style, players and the development of the team.

To say that this decision was out of left field would be an understatement. The appointment of Houllier did have merit though. His most recent job prior to Liverpool had been as Technical Director of the French Football Federation, where he'd been given mich credit for France winning the World Cup only a week earlier. It had originally been thought to appoint Houllier as Director of Football, but the board felt that this wouldn't give him the time with the players that they wanted. Conversely, Roy Evans had originally believed that Houllier was being contracted to replace the outgoing legendary coach Ronnie Moran. It's easy to see why this was doomed to fail. The arrangement was never going to work.

Nevertheless, with two managers, Liverpool headed into the transfer window looking to improve their squad. The first incoming player was Sean Dundee, a South Africa-born striker who was highly regarded in Germany, having played for Karlsruher SC, who had been relegated from the Bundesliga in 1997/98. In the previous two seasons, Dundee had scored 33 goals in 61 matches. He was signed for a fee of £1.8m to provide cover for the still injured Robbie Fowler alongside starlet Michael Owen. Also (re)arriving at Liverpool was defender Steve Staunton, who signed on a free after his contract expired at Aston Villa, returning to the club that he left in August 1991 after being sold by Graeme Souness. Staunton's return offered class and experience, but the Irish international was no longer the player he'd been. The final signing of the summer was Norwegian right-sided player Vegard Heggem, who was brought in for £3.5m from Rosenborg. He was the main signing that both Houllier and Evans had agreed on, but the joint managers couldn't decide on where they wanted to play him. Ominous indeed. For comparison, Manchester

United signed Jaap Stam and Dwight Yorke as their headline summer acquisitions, while Arsenal signed Freddie Ljungberg.

Leaving the club was Australian Nick Rizzo, who was signed by Crystal Palace for £300,000, having never made an appearance for the Reds. Also departing Anfield was Neil Ruddock, who left after five seasons and 152 matches. 'Razor' had experienced a poor 1997/98 season and was signed by West Ham United for £400,000. The final name to leave that summer was Michael Thomas, who joined Benfica on a free transfer. He'd been an important – if rotated – part of Liverpool's central midfield over the past few seasons, eventually losing his place with the return to form and fitness of Jamie Redknapp. Thomas played for the club in seven league campaigns and a total of 163 matches in the famous red shirt.

The Evans/Houllier tenure began with a journey south to Hampshire to face Southampton at The Dell. The first combined selection was Friedel, Heggem, Carragher, Babb, Staunton, McManaman, McAteer, Ince, Berger, Owen and Riedle. Patrik Berger was receiving his first start for some time in place of Øyvind Leonhardsen, who was on the bench. McAteer also returned to central midfield, the role he'd attracted attention in while playing for Bolton Wanderers in the First Division. However, it was Michael Owen – coming off his star-making performance at the 1998 World

Cup and now wearing the No. 10 shirt – who created Liverpool's first goal of the season, moving out to the left-hand side and sending a pinpoint cross into the box for Karl-Heinz Riedle to meet with his head and power the ball past Paul Jones in the Saints' goal. The German striker's goal brought Liverpool level, and it was Owen who secured the win, pouncing on some poor defending from a long throw by Steve Staunton to blast the ball into the net from five yards out. For a first performance of the season, Liverpool looked good. Owen was as sharp as he'd been the previous season, Staunton looked secure at left-back and Heggem grew into the match, causing problems when attacking from right-back. What's more, Phil Babb and Jamie Carragher looked secure in the back line. Positive signs for the British/French alliance at Anfield.

After a 0-0 draw with reigning Premier League champions Arsenal in their next league match, things looked even better eight days later when they travelled to Newcastle, where Ruud Gullit had just taken over from Kenny Dalglish. Michael Owen – celebrating after signing a new, £20,000-a-week, five-year contract with the club – tore the Geordie defence to shreds, scoring a wonderful first-half hat-trick that demonstrated his sheer class, finishing ability and lightning pace. The first was a not-so-easy tap-in after Paul Ince's shot from distance had been parried towards the edge of the box and Owen simply fired the ball quickly back into the goal. His second saw him beat the offside trap to receive the ball from Steve McManaman, before coolly waiting for Shay Given to make his move and side-footing the ball past the Irish keeper into the net. Owen's hat-trick was completed after some careless passing from the Newcastle defence allowed Karl-Heinz Riedle to get a toe in, the ball falling to Owen, who simply outran the defenders, before effortlessly nudging the ball into the far corner with the outside of his right foot as Given came out to challenge him – getting nowhere near the ball.

If you want to see how truly terrifying Michael Owen was at this point to any Premier League defence, just watch his performance in this first half. He showed undeniable confidence, unmatched pace and natural finishing ability. Liverpool made it four just before half-time when Patrik Berger celebrated his return by firing the ball into the bottom corner from 20 yards after evading two Newcastle tacklers. Gullit's Newcastle did score in the first half through Stéphane Guivarc'h, but it was a dominant performance from the Reds that sent them top of the table.

As August moved into September, Liverpool won again, against Coventry City at Anfield, Berger opening the scoring in the 26th minute and Jamie Redknapp making it two following a lucky deflection after he shot from the edge of the box. In more good news, Steve McManaman told reporters that a deal was on the way to remain at the club, and Robbie Fowler returned to the pitch, scoring six times in a friendly against Wrexham. If Liverpool could get Fowler and Owen firing together, the pairing could win them their first league title since 1989/90 under Kenny Dalglish. If.

Infuriatingly, Liverpool then went on a winless run until the end of October. It started with a 2-1 loss at Upton Park against West Ham United that only looked close because of Karl-Heinz Riedle's 87th-minute goal following a Jason McAteer cross. Liverpool selected Steve Harkness for the match, with Michael Owen the only real striker in the line-up, and they paid dearly for it, dropping off the top spot and never coming close to it again all season. The decision to select Harkness had been Houllier's, with Riedle dropped to fit him into the team. Evans was vindicated when Riedle scored after coming on as a substitute. The honeymoon was well and truly over for the Evans and Houllier partnership, as their differences became clearer, the pair disagreed more often – although always remaining cordial with one another – and players were unsure of who to go to and who was really in charge at the club.

One positive amid this poor league run was the sequence of victories in Europe, as Liverpool began their UEFA Cup campaign with 3-0 and 5-0 wins over Slovakian club Košice. The first leg saw Fowler return to first-team action as a substitute, then in the second leg he partnered Owen up front. However, the shocking league form included a 3-3 draw with Charlton Athletic at Anfield, which saw Robbie Fowler score twice on his league return – the first a penalty, the second a scrambled finish on the goal line – but it was Liverpool's defence that let them down. Phil Babb came in for most of the criticism, being booed off by the Anfield faithful after a terrible performance. Changes were made in the defence ahead of the next match, against none other than Manchester United. Jason McAteer played at right-back instead of Vegard Heggem, Stig Inge Bjørnebye came in at left-back, and Brad Friedel was dropped, with David James returning between the sticks. Karl-Heinz Riedle partnered Michael Owen up front, with Robbie Fowler not quite fit enough. Unfortunately for Reds fans, Roy Keane and Paul Scholes controlled the midfield zone with and without the ball, meaning Owen and Riedle had precious little to feed upon, and goals from Denis Irwin and Scholes secured a relatively easy 2-0 win for United, who were looking to reclaim their crown in 1998/99. They would, emphatically.

October began with three straight draws for the Reds, the first on 4 October against Chelsea at Anfield, with a Jamie Redknapp free kick cancelling out a Pierluigi Casiraghi goal that a sliding Phil Babb had just managed not to prevent – yes, *that one*. He was later replaced by Dominic Matteo in defence. The match also became famous for featuring a clash between captain Paul Ince and Chelsea's Graeme Le Saux that was described as a verbal confrontation and part of the game. Thirteen days later, following the international break, Liverpool once again failed to win a Merseyside derby, with Michael Owen looking tired and rumours of a Bosman transfer once again surrounding Steve McManaman, with the discussed contract from the previous months still not yet signed. The final draw of the three was in Europe, as Liverpool drew 0-0 at home with Valencia in the first leg of the second round of the UEFA Cup.

Delightfully, Liverpool then ended their winless run in the league by thrashing Nottingham Forest 5-1 at Anfield, with Michael Owen scoring four, being partnered by Karl-Heinz Riedle, with Robbie Fowler on the bench. It's easy to say looking back now, but it's evident that Owen worked better with someone alongside him who would do the running and passing for him, allowing him to use his blistering pace and dribbling ability to get beyond the defence. Liverpool then won again three days later in the League Cup third round, 3-1 at home to Fulham, with Fowler getting on the scoresheet and Sean Dundee making his debut for the club. At this point, there were already rumours that he would be leaving, not meeting the club's standards both on and off the pitch. The victory would prove to be Roy Evans's last as manager of Liverpool Football Club.

October ended with Liverpool being beaten 1-0 by Leicester City at Filbert Street after another poor performance that saw Leicester's Kasey Keller make only two saves in the whole 90 minutes. To add further insult to injury, Jason McAteer was sent off in the 86th minute for a second bookable offence, and he wouldn't play for a Roy Evans team again. Indeed, McAteer wouldn't play for the club many more times at all. Evans's post-match press conference was deliberately extremely brief as pressure mounted on him and Gérard Houllier. Despite the poor run of form, the Reds were still fourth in the table, six points behind early front-runners Aston Villa.

Liverpool's next fixture was the second leg of their UEFA Cup second-round tie against Valencia. In a tense tie in Spain, they managed to hold on to a 2-2 draw to win the tie on away goals, with Steve McManaman and Patrik Berger scoring in the 81st and 86th minutes to cancel out Claudio López's 45th-minute strike and nullify David James's unlucky own goal in the 90th minute as a free kick came off the post and hit him on the back before trickling over the line. Both Paul Ince and Steve McManaman received their marching orders late on following a scuffle that began with McManaman and Amadeo Carboni, but Liverpool were able to keep their cool. In reality, Valencia could have won 4-2 with the chances they had in the first half, but poor finishing and excellent keeping by David James cost them victory.

After this match, Evans and Houllier fell out over a decision by Houllier to give some of the Liverpool shirts away. In the hours after the match, Roy Evans decided that he would hand in his notice.

Liverpool's next two matches saw a poor 2-1 defeat to Derby County at Anfield, with Jamie Redknapp scoring late to make the scoreline look respectable. After the match, Roy Evans started to show his true feelings, saying that he and Gérard Houllier were doing the job to the best of their ability and that it was for other people to make a decision. The defeat saw Liverpool drop to 11th, nine points off the top. Three days later, they were again beaten, this time 3-1 in the League Cup fourth round by Tottenham Hotspur. Liverpool's only goal was scored, of course, by Michael Owen. However, he suffered the first of many hamstring injuries while netting the consolation goal.

Two days later, on 12 November 1998, Roy Evans officially resigned as joint manager of Liverpool Football Club. A joint announcement was made between Evans and chairman David Moores that he would be leaving the club rather than taking up another position within the hierarchy, and that Gérard Houllier would now assume the position of manager. Evans stated that he didn't feel that his record at the club was one of failure, but that at a club with the records, history and prestige of Liverpool, anything that isn't victory is deemed as a failure. He made it clear that there were no issues between him and Gérard Houllier, that the joint manager arrangement simply didn't work for the players, and that the decision was being made for the betterment of the club, to give Houllier a chance to work on his own with the players.

Evans believed that his best moment as manager was winning the Coca-Cola Cup in 1994/95. However, to reduce his tenure as manager of the Reds to just one match and one trophy would be unfair to a man who did so much for Liverpool Football Club. A man who recovered and then maintained the standards that had been lost over the previous few years. As Roy Evans exited stage left, Gérard Houllier announced the return of Phil Thompson to the club as his assistant manager, while David Moores said that the club had to continue moving forward. As always, though, with Liverpool Football Club, you never walk alone.

Chapter 9

Evans's Liverpool Post-Evans

GÉRARD HOULLIER'S first match in sole charge of Liverpool Football Club was against big-spending Leeds United at Anfield. Robbie Fowler opened the scoring for the Reds in the 68th minute with a penalty, but Houllier's team would then capitulate to a 3-1 loss through goals from Alan Smith and a brace by Jimmy Floyd Hasselbaink. The defeat showed there were clearly issues, which would take time and significant changes to be resolved.

The remainder of the season would see Liverpool largely meander along – and Michael Owen suffer his first serious hamstring injury in the return fixture against Leeds later in the year at Elland Road – to finish seventh in the table, 25 points off the pace, as rivals Manchester United recorded the first league, FA Cup and Champions League treble, confirming their dynasty as the team of the 1990s. Liverpool would bounce back over the coming years, finishing fourth in 1999/00 and winning their own treble in 2000/01 as they secured the League Cup, FA Cup and UEFA Cup. However, they were now largely unrecognisable from Evans's team of the 1990s, as Houllier looked to alter the squad, bringing in a significant foreign contingent in names such as Christian Ziege, Sami Hyypiä and Dietmar Hamann. It would take time – and another manager – for Liverpool to regain their position as a European and domestic power, finishing second in 2001/02, and making two Champions League finals in 2004/05 and 2006/07, winning the first in a memorable night for the club in Istanbul.

While Roy Evans may have said during his farewell press conference that the best moment of his career was the Coca-Cola Cup triumph in 1994/95, to reduce his time as manager to one single final is too dismissive. When he took up the role of manager in late January 1994, the club was in turmoil after Graeme Souness and almost unrecognisable from the club that Souness himself had played for, both in terms of style and achievements. Evans restored a swagger and style that made them rightly a club that was loved by neutrals throughout the 1990s. For sure, they could have been more defensively sound and they could have been more consistent in big matches, but they repeatedly showed that they were more than capable of hanging with the big clubs of the era: Manchester United, Blackburn Rovers, Newcastle United and Arsenal. Often, it isn't the serial winners in football that are the best remembered, but the most interesting and most attractive, and Roy Evans's Liverpool were certainly that. They may have been remembered as the 'Spice Boys' for their off-field antics and lapses in professionalism – the passing of a pound coin from player to player during a match is hard to defend – but this was also a harsh characterisation of a collection of young players who were catapulted to superstardom at Liverpool and enjoyed many of the off-field activities that occurred at many other top clubs.

Under Roy Evans, a whole generation of young players came through that would go on to have successful careers in English football and beyond. The two players that his team will always be associated with – Robbie Fowler and Steve McManaman – both went on to have fantastic careers. McManaman would eventually leave on his much-rumoured Bosman transfer, joining Spanish giants Real Madrid and going on to form a key part of their midfield for their eighth European Cup/Champions League victory against Valencia, as well as coming off the bench for their ninth against Bayer Leverkusen at Hampden Park. McManaman's playing career is often forgotten, but he should be rightly remembered as one of the most talented midfielders of his generation and one of the most creative players ever to wear the famous red shirt of Liverpool. Robbie Fowler, so often the lethal striker who saved Liverpool in the 90s, was never truly the same after the awful knee injury that ended his

1997/98 season, but he remained a top finisher, joining Leeds United in 2001 and Manchester City in 2003, before enjoying an emotional return to Liverpool in 2006 under Rafael Benítez. He is rightfully remembered as a Kop legend, a Merseyside lad who gave everything for the red shirt and was at one point up there with Alan Shearer as the most dangerous English striker in the Premier League. His seemingly effortless finishing ability was a joy to witness for all at Anfield.

Future Liverpool legends also gained their first starts under Evans. Michael Owen, who would go on to become one of the world's most sought-after strikers, broke into the team in 1997/98 and went on to dazzle the footballing world with his unbelievable pace, ability to run with the ball at speed and finishing ability. Injuries would damage Owen's career – and hamstrings – meaning he remains one of English football's great 'what ifs', but he was given his start in the team by Roy Evans. Jamie Carragher, who would go on to become another Anfield legend and a rock in central defence, gained his early appearances under Evans and was a significant contributor in the inconsistent back four of 1997/98. It could never be said that Roy Evans didn't give the young players at Melwood a chance, and many of them would go on to prove him right to do so over the rest of their careers.

There were also others such as Jamie Redknapp and Stig Inge Bjørnebye who owed a part recovery of their careers to Evans. Redknapp broke into the team under Graeme Souness in late 1991 but began to plateau, receiving only intermittent starts and suffering from the lack of style that the team developed in the later period of Souness's reign. Under Evans, he turned into a fine passing central-midfielder, one that was likely decades ahead of his time and would be celebrated in the modern game. Bjørnebye had suffered a difficult start at Liverpool but was reborn following Evans's decision to switch to a back three, being utilised as a left wing-back, encouraged to go forward and put in crosses for the strikers. He was appropriately rewarded for his play when he was chosen in the PFA Team of the Year following the 1996/97 season. The switch to 3-5-2 also served the original right wing-back well, when Rob Jones was named right-back in the PFA Team of the Year for 1994/95. There are many others who should give Evans credit for his role in either developing or helping to recover their careers, such as Mark Wright, John Scales and Michael Thomas.

Evans also provided dignified endings to Liverpool legends such as Ian Rush and John Barnes. Rush enjoyed a career swansong as a secondary gunner alongside Robbie Fowler before leaving to join Leeds United and eventually Kenny Dalglish's Newcastle United. John Barnes, who had often been criticised by Graeme Souness, adapted his game under the instruction of Evans and became a gifted central-midfielder, confident on the ball, able to take it under pressure and capable of making the right passes into the attacking zones of the pitch. Barnes had noticeably regressed as a player under Souness due to many factors – one of which was injuries – but under Evans he received his last England cap in 1995 and was a key part of Liverpool's thrilling 1995/96 team that won the hearts and minds of fans across the country.

Most importantly, Roy Evans had made Liverpool *Liverpool* again. Yes, they'd needed change and modernisation in the rapidly changing world of the Premier League when Gérard Houllier officially took over as manager in November 1998, but Evans had restored a heart to Liverpool that had appeared to be vanishing in the early 90s. They were once again a top team in English football, a team that played with a passing style that was reminiscent of – if not as successful as – many of the great Liverpool teams of the 70s and 80s, and captured the hearts of the Kop and all around Anfield.

Roy Evans may only have won the Coca-Cola Cup as manager but he did far more for the football club on a larger scale, ensuring that it continued to be loved, respected and identifiable as Liverpool Football Club. Without the work that he did as manager throughout the mid- to late-1990s, they wouldn't be what they are today. It's easy to assume that Liverpool would always be *Liverpool*, but historic examples such as Leeds United, Nottingham Forest, Blackburn Rovers and

Derby County suggest otherwise. A worrying trend had developed at Anfield of mediocrity and average football, and Roy Evans, as one of the last remaining members of the famous and fabled boot room, did his job in returning the club to prominence. Regardless of titles and cups, he should be rightly and fondly remembered by all who wear red on Merseyside as the manager who prevented a potential downfall and kept the heart and soul of the football club alive, then respectfully stepped aside when he'd gone as far as he could. From January 1994 to November 1998, Roy Evans gave English football one of its most remembered and celebrated teams, and he deserves all the credit in the world for that. Simply, Liverpool Football Club might not be the titan it is today without Roy Evans. Perhaps just a little less spice might have been required. Viva Forever.

Bibliography

Select Bibliography

Blows, K., *Terminator: Authorised Julian Dicks Story* (Polar Print Group, 1996).

Ellis, M. & Souness, G., *Souness: The Management Years* (Andre Deutsch, 1999).

Evans, T., *I Don't Know What It Is but I Love It: Liverpool's Unforgettable 1983–84 Season* (Penguin, 2015).

Grobbelaar, B., *Life in a Jungle* (deCoubertin Books, 2018).

Hughes, S., *Men in White Suits: Liverpool FC in the 1990s – The Players' Stories* (Bantam Press, 2015).

Wilson, J., *Inverting the Pyramid: The History of Football Tactics* (Orion UK, 2014).

Select Webography

https://anfieldindex.com/

https://bleacherreport.com/

https://www.football365.com/

https://www.lfchistory.net/
https://www.premierleague.com/
https://www.skysports.com/
http://www.sporting-heroes.net/
http://stadiumdb.com/
https://www.the42.ie/
Official club website of Liverpool Football Club

Select Newspapers/Magazines

The Guardian
The Herald
The Independent
Liverpool Echo
Stoke Sentinel